Good Mourning
a collection of aches and ecstasy

Good Mourning

a collection of aches and ecstasy

Brenda Baker

All rights reserved. No part of this publication may be reproduced in whole or in part or stored in a retrieval system or transmitted in any form or by any means, electronic, mechanical, photocopying, recording, or otherwise, without written permission of the author and publisher of the book.

For information regarding permission, contact Inkwell Imprint @ www.inkwellimprint.com

ISBN-13: 978-1-7322868-9-4

Library of Congress Control Number: 2024913918

Published by Inkwell Imprint

Copyright © 2024 Brenda Baker
All rights reserved.

To the parts of love,

To the parts of loss,

And all the bits between.

Thank you.

Come Inside

Farmland	2
Prolong	4
Drip	6
Spark of Fervor	7
Dandelion Rainbow	10
Acreage of You	12
Tied and Tidy	14
Accumulation	16
Summons	18
Eyes to the Sky	20
Kairos Clock	22
Yes, Please	24
Buried At Sea	26
Ambit	27
Autumn Allows	30
Sealed and Concealed	32
Sunny	34
Universe	36
Atrophy	37
Tranquil Touch	40
Layover	42
Lullaby	44

Supine and Prepared	46
Soaked	47
Innocence Disbarred	50
Flourish	52
Leave the Gate	54
The Archives	56
Sanctuary	57
Nibble	60
Sanctity	61
Seascapes and Scandal	64
Reclamation Place	66
Evening Envelopes	68
'Til Death Do Us Part	70
Linger	72
An Inside Inquisition	74
Knitting Strings	76
The Storm	77
Tuesdays	80
A Deliberate Devotion	82
Template to Contemplate	84
Tracks	86
Limitless	87
Canvas	90
Abide	92
The Builder	94

Promenade for Two	96
Present	97
Tender Topography	100
Refuse	102
So, Stay	103
Twilight Stroll	106
Reservations	108
Lust and Line	110
Apex Trance	112
Carnal Cuisine	114
Leap	116
An Evening's Pass	118
All the Way Down	120
Last Supper	122
Soothe	124
Breathe	125
Radar	128
Supper Club	130
Yoga Tempo	132
Pursue; in due time	133
The Morning Always Comes	136
Noun of Safety	138
Thank You Notes	140
The Permission of Watermelon	141
On Delay	144

The Gardener	146
A Pause	147
Surplus	150
Mirage	152
Provisions	154
Book of You	155
Repent	158
Captain	159
Unearth	162
Tiger Shark	164
Silent Stories	166
The Dichotomy of You and Me	167
Candlelight	170

Good Mourning

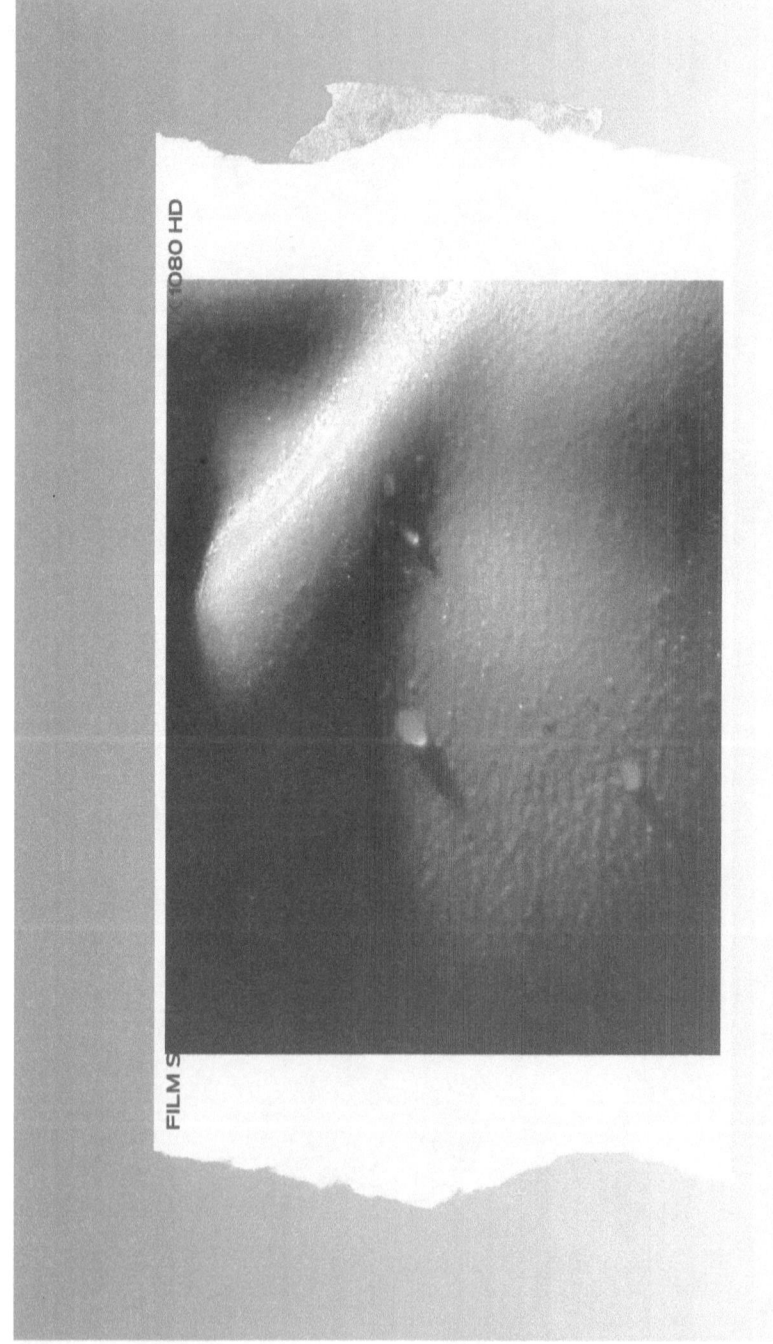

Farmland

They could sense
He held more than a key
He owned the territories
The miles of her
Once wild and free
Now sat
Illuminated
In the afterglow
Of how he loved
Her
And
As daylight
Places tired
Responsibilities
Into capable embrace of night
That feeds the fire
Her fields listen
To his rain
And skilled hands
That planted
More than
Seeds
To harvest

Good Mourning

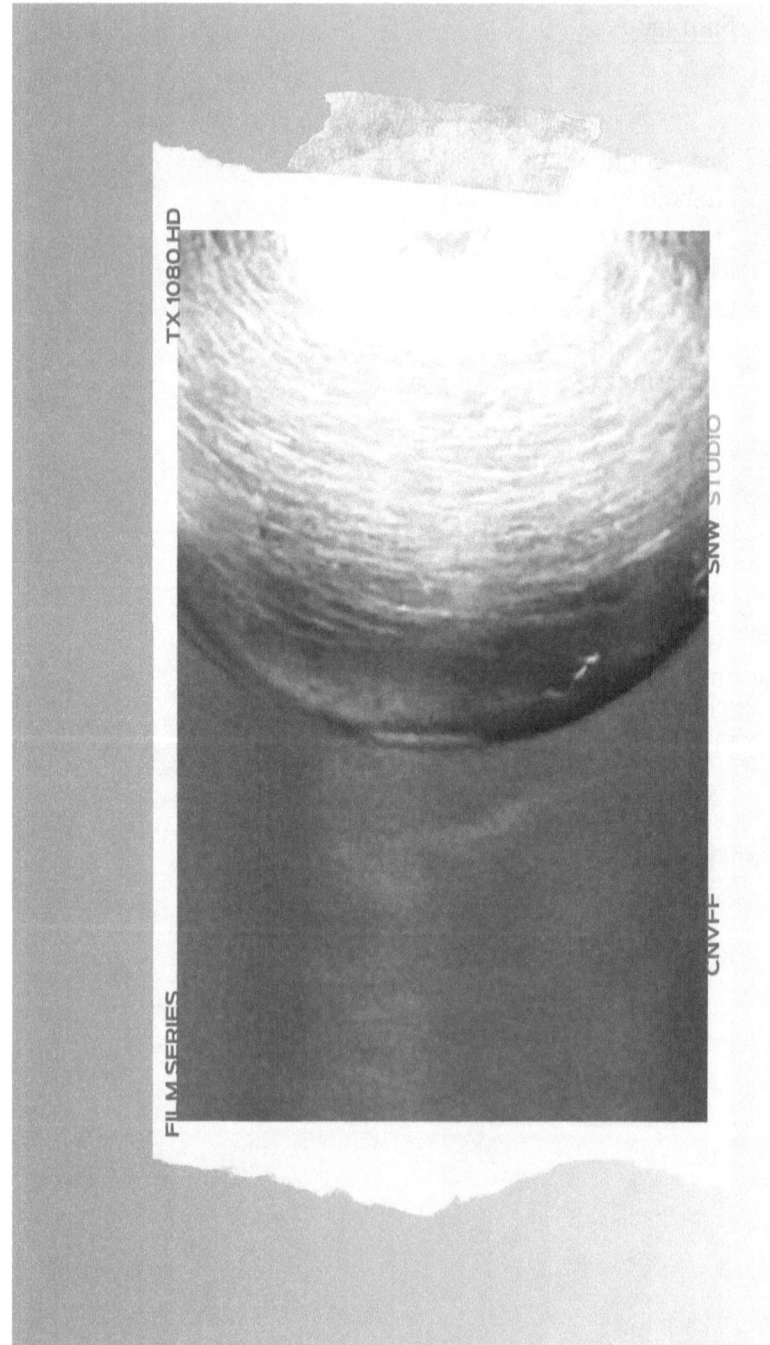

Prolong

It's not so much
Trepidation
As it is
Anticipation
Of entering her room
Smudged and coy
Palo santo
On the mantle and
Incense in
The fireplace
With a place to
Lay it all bare
Right in the middle
As she waits to
Feast
A hearty repast
Whispering invitation
By way
Of that slide of hand
With a grip that
Lasts
Murmuring
This will last
A long, long while

Good Mourning

Drip

Come
Here
And lay your hands
Where they belong
Along the curve
Of my soft
Impatient lips
Where you
First noticed
A bead of sweat
That had nothing
To do
With
The summer heat

Spark of Fervor

Eyes dipping low
In submissive
Posture
But there is no submission
Anywhere in sight
An ache so deep
Will never be subdued
With passive exchange
Of glances
It becomes a countdown
Of anticipation
Breaths
And exhalations
Murmuring suggestions of coffee
And time
And the unspoken
Palpable space
Between words
Fills up worlds
With the curvature of
Your lips
And my tongue
Tracing where you've been
Where I won't question
Choices you've made
Or
Moments prior
To the ones
We fill
With fingers in deep

As you learn my hips
And pressure builds

Good Mourning

Dandelion Rainbow

Captured once
And let go twice
She sits
Still as a student
Still like a statue
As wind blows
Past
Past sorrow
Pulls it up
Up and away
And sows it for her
To send seeds
To greener pastures
They're out there
Somewhere
Her soft eyes will wait
For the rain
While a tender heart
Coaxes blooms
Only dreams can see

Good Mourning

Acreage of You

Let it be slow
With space to build
And pulse
Let it fill my thoughts
My veins
My hopes and
Dreams
Let those fingers
Take
Their
Time
With me
I long to lounge in this
Sun filled field
With nothing to tend
But these easy thoughts
And your gentle
Eyes
That know
How I like my coffee

Good Mourning

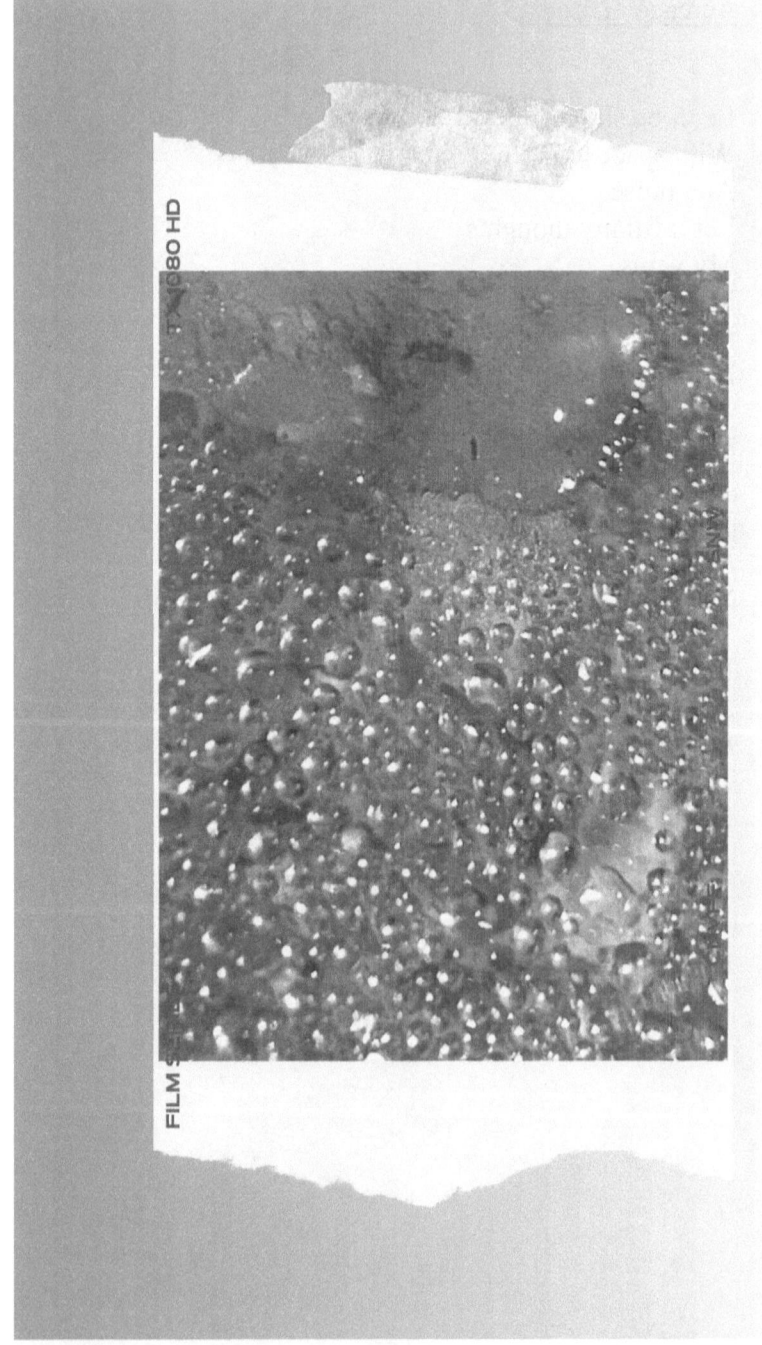

Tied and Tidy

You've been on my mind
Still
And in my bones still
And I can't seem to find
The rag
To wipe it
Clean
Clean slate
Clean it up
Clean and tidy
But I long for
Your sweet, simple victory
In the thick of
This fog
That clouds
My vision

Good Mourning

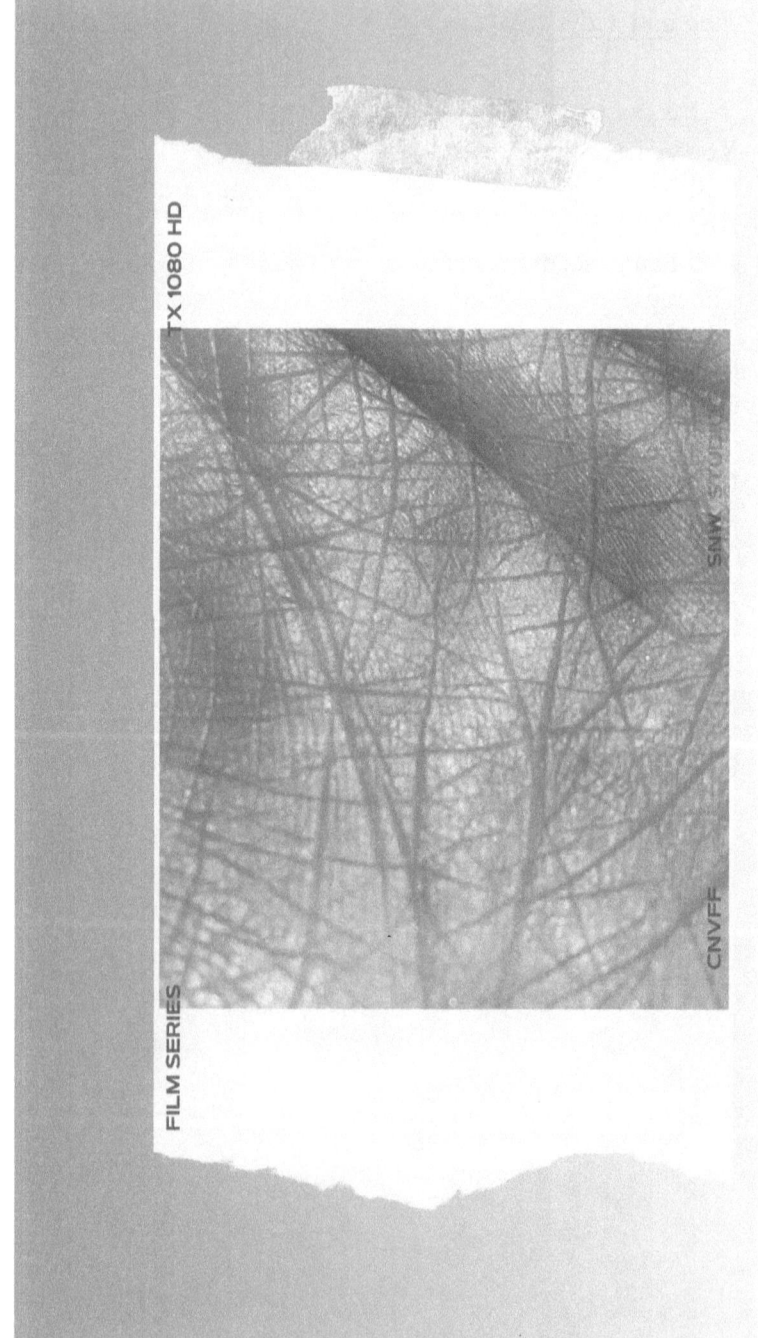

Accumulation

When he wants to play with me
I am helpless
His eyes change
Posture eases
Lengthens
A slight variation to the outsider
But I know this move
I am this move
Softening of the gaze
An invitation to casual exchange
When our eyes meet
Time releases itself
For time is an irrelevant thing
While tracing the jawline
Of an eager man
And sounds of the ordinary
That pass through
Numb ears of others
Without regard
Slice my unsteady rhythm
To expose my
Heart
Recalling countless breaths
That filled
This chest
And paused the spinning
Of the earth
Itself

Good Mourning

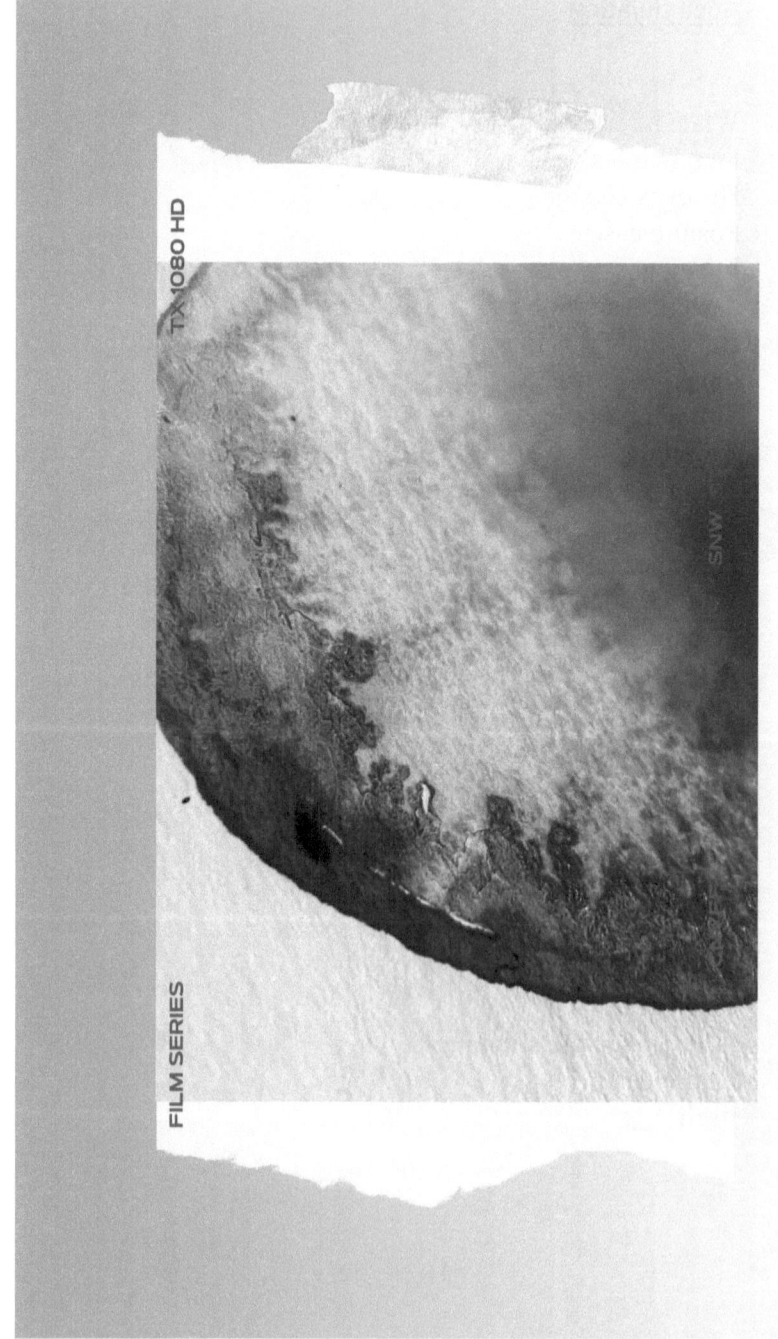

Summons

Images
Of your lips
Trapse about
These thoughts
And time halts
While I gaze ahead
A soft glaze
Sets the tone
A rousing vision
Obsessed on
Obtaining
That sweet nectar of your smile
Against my collarbone
While tender palms
Explore
Passageways
Reserved for lovers
With intention
For more than simply
Skin
To
Skin
An intoxicating
Concoction
Conducts
An assault
Of sensations
And extends
An invitation
To play

Good Mourning

Eyes to the Sky

It's been
The same moon
This whole time
As the sun shined
And clouds cried
As fields bloomed
And bucket lists sat
In their keeper's dreams
Still full to the brim
As a merciless clock
Ticked down
With impossible
Unpredictable
Pace
And baby swans
Took their first
Swim
This whole time
She shines
Look up, darling
She shines for you

Good Mourning

Kairos Clock

She'll pause time
For you
For a moment
For a lifetime
And your lungs will relax
To primal pace
As heartbeats keep
Rhythm with the seasons
Not the time clock
As she sings you
To sleep
In arms that know
The fight
And choose
The garden

Good Mourning

Yes, Please

Will you tuck me in
With firm hand
And soft song
As the night does
What night does best?
What she likes best is
To craft
An easy canvas
For stories
To spread those verbs
Like you spread my legs
And capture my attention
With
Your
Intention
And interjection
As preludes
To morning pancakes
Set the stage and
Hopes of eternal summer mornings
Laced with fiery promise
Run rampant
In the cavernous echoes
Between my ears
Lay me down softly, then
And kiss me with
A lifetime of love

Good Mourning

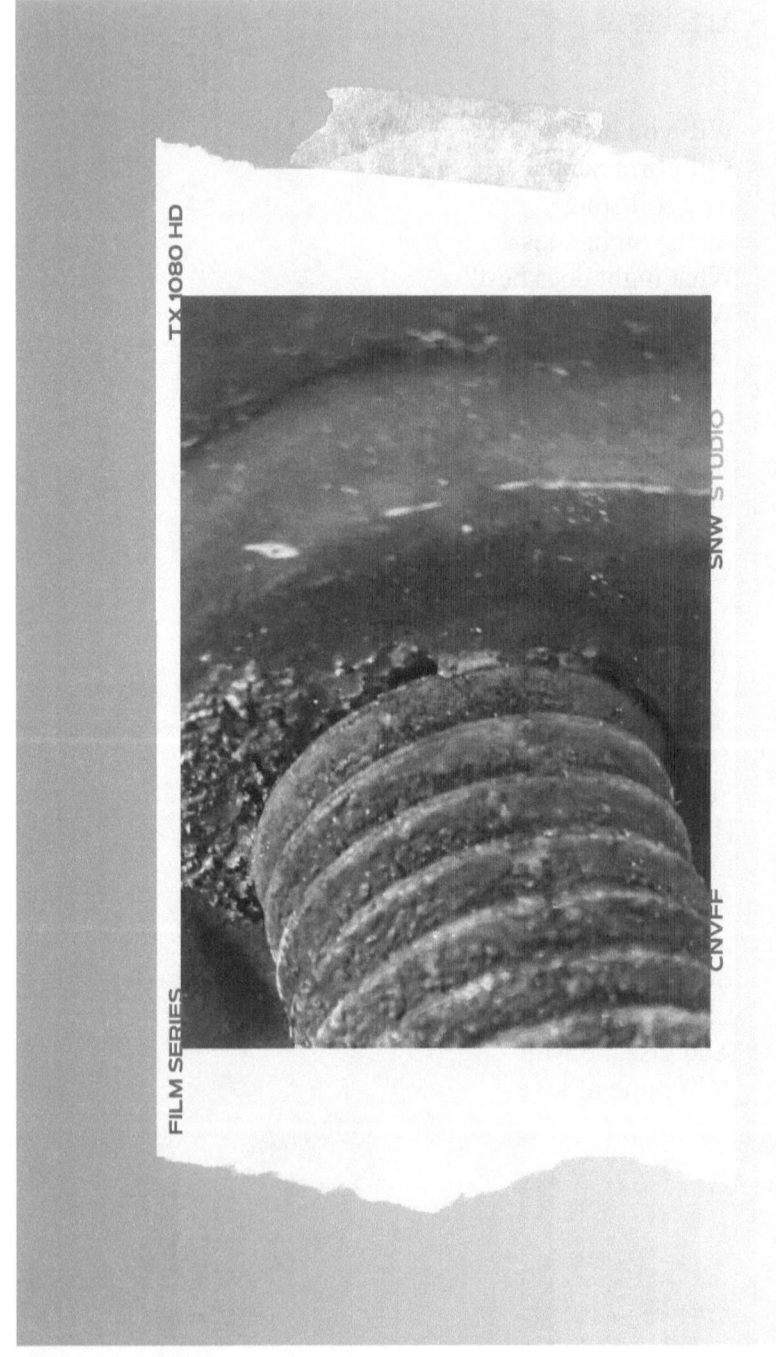

Buried At Sea

I've toiled
In soil
To envelope
Parts of you
Wrapped in gauze
A tender secret
Stained plum
With blistered knuckles
Tired of the fight
But wary of the yield
To yield
And finally
Give it up
To the ghost who
Carries past reasons
To the surf
And calls it all
Back to sea

Ambit

Engulfing
Vision
Of worldly sights
As you
Tower
Above me
And I stare up
To your stars
In awe of
Acquiring
The presence
You possess
Eyes commanding
Demanding
My focus
Without a word
Without a move
Desires
Exchange between
Curious thoughts
This tension
Crossing thresholds
And boundaries
While caution
Is laid to bed
Like
How you've
Laid
Me
Hold me

Steady
Locked eyes
On my horizon
That watch you search
The signs
For permission
To
Proceed

Good Mourning

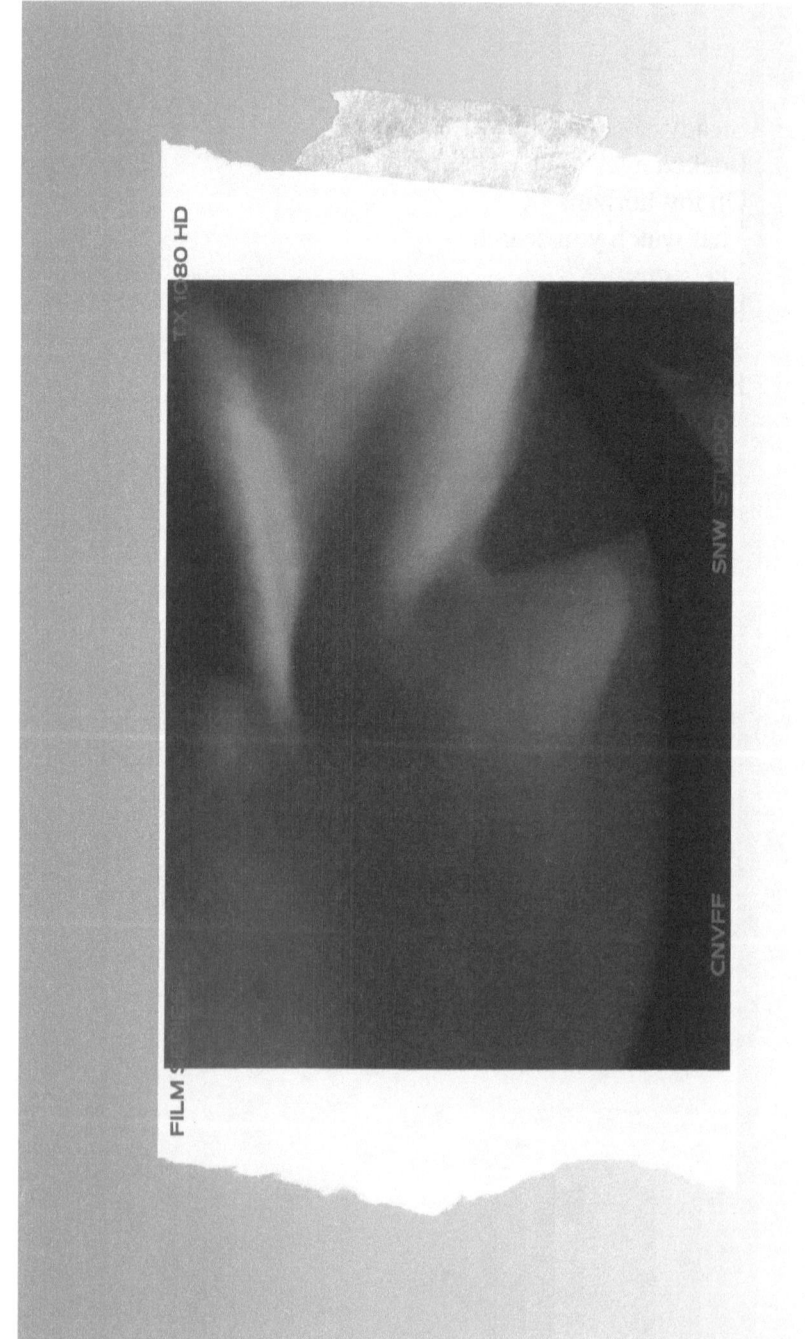

Autumn Allows

Early
Pumpkin colored skies
Invite longer
Embrace
Where lips taste
Of sleepy Saturday mornings
Unkempt and long
Warm
And easy
Coffee after coffee
That spills
Into afternoon
Tea
And
Bites of
Something good to eat
For sharing
The whole day
Slips by
And skies
Return
To shades
Of calm
While hands slip
Into
Sacred spaces

Good Mourning

Sealed and Concealed

Supplement the craving
And succumb
To what covers
Your hide
As you
Hide
In plain view
With dreams that
Scream
In the
Early morning
And rouse you
From dangerous sleep
Alone
Again
Alone and safe
Where your
One way
Is
The only way
But this truth of life
Craves
To feel it all
To blister and burn
Erupt and settle down
In the dust
Of your desert
Raked clean of debris
Swept clean to hide
Sins
Within

Good Mourning

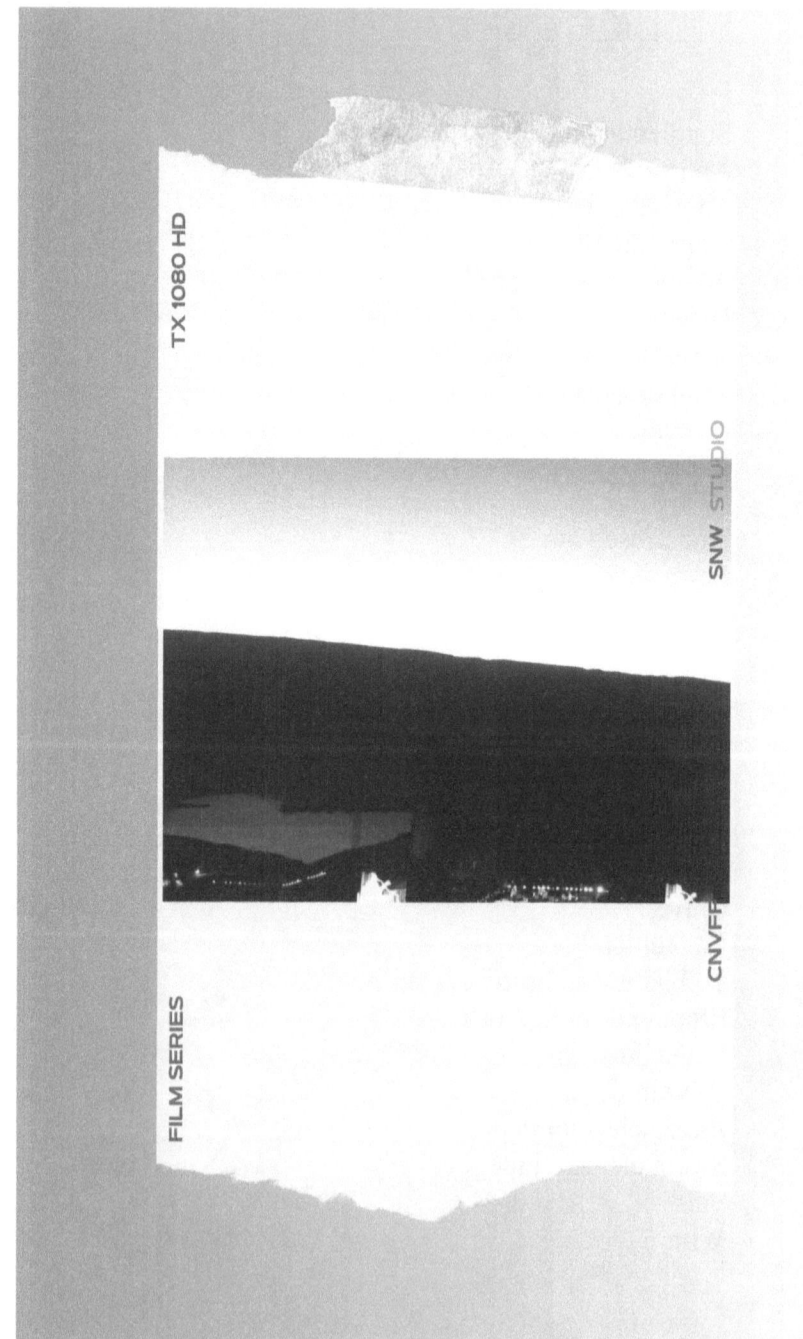

Sunny

If it's easy, then
Not a chase
To be caught
Not a prize to be won
Not like that, anyway
Where lips meet comfort
Of
Familiar requests
Embroidered in the mind
Of a generous lover
Not complacent
Nor compliant
Casual
A slow beat
That fills the evenings with
Tea for two
And an eager mouth
For that tongue
Those fingers
That girth that slips
In soft places
Just so
With your name
Etched deep
And a caravan
For two

Good Mourning

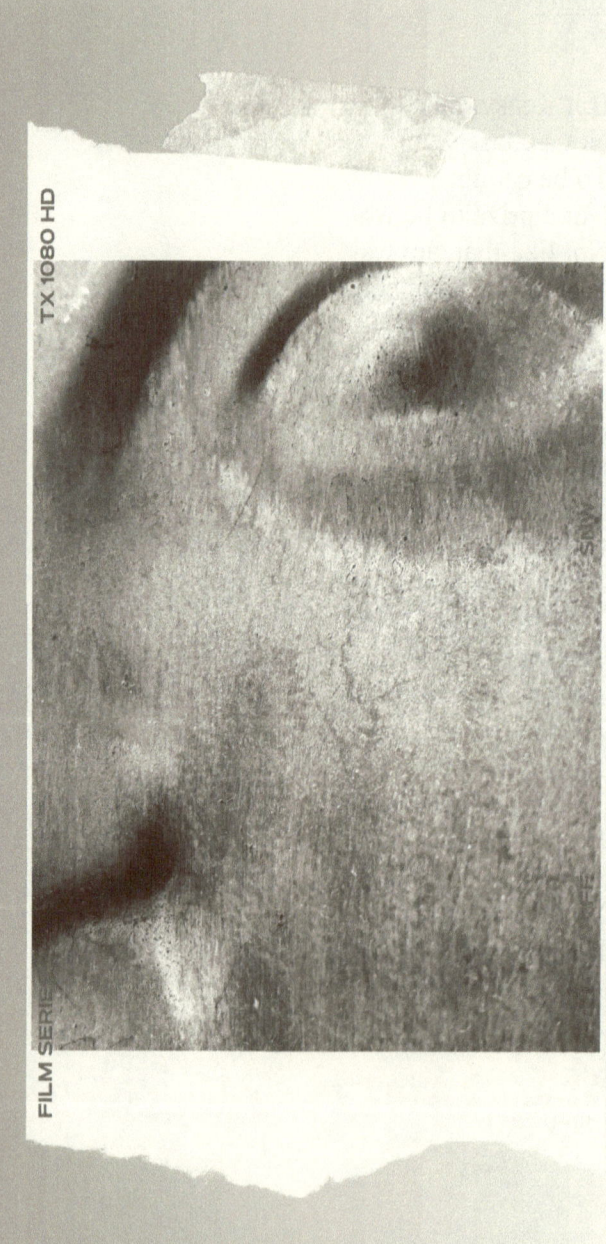

Universe

She held the sorrow
For the world
Tucked inside
Closed lips
And
Eyes that made
The rain

Atrophy

And so I wonder, then
What will become
Of the words
Once dripping from tongues
Of anticipation
Greeted by a greedy lover
With ears so soft
Like fine velvet
Poised
In wait
But days pass on
And seasons shift
Shifting
Wilting words
Once wild and quick wit
Heady with fragrant nose
And interlude
Cast wayside
Now flat, flat as stale air
Abandoned with no reprieve
Littered
Scattered
Scavenged for
Cascading notes
Mixed with salt
From the tears
Of a solitary lover
Those words
Inaudible and crass

Flood spaces
Once filled with promise
Hold promise
Of none

Good Mourning

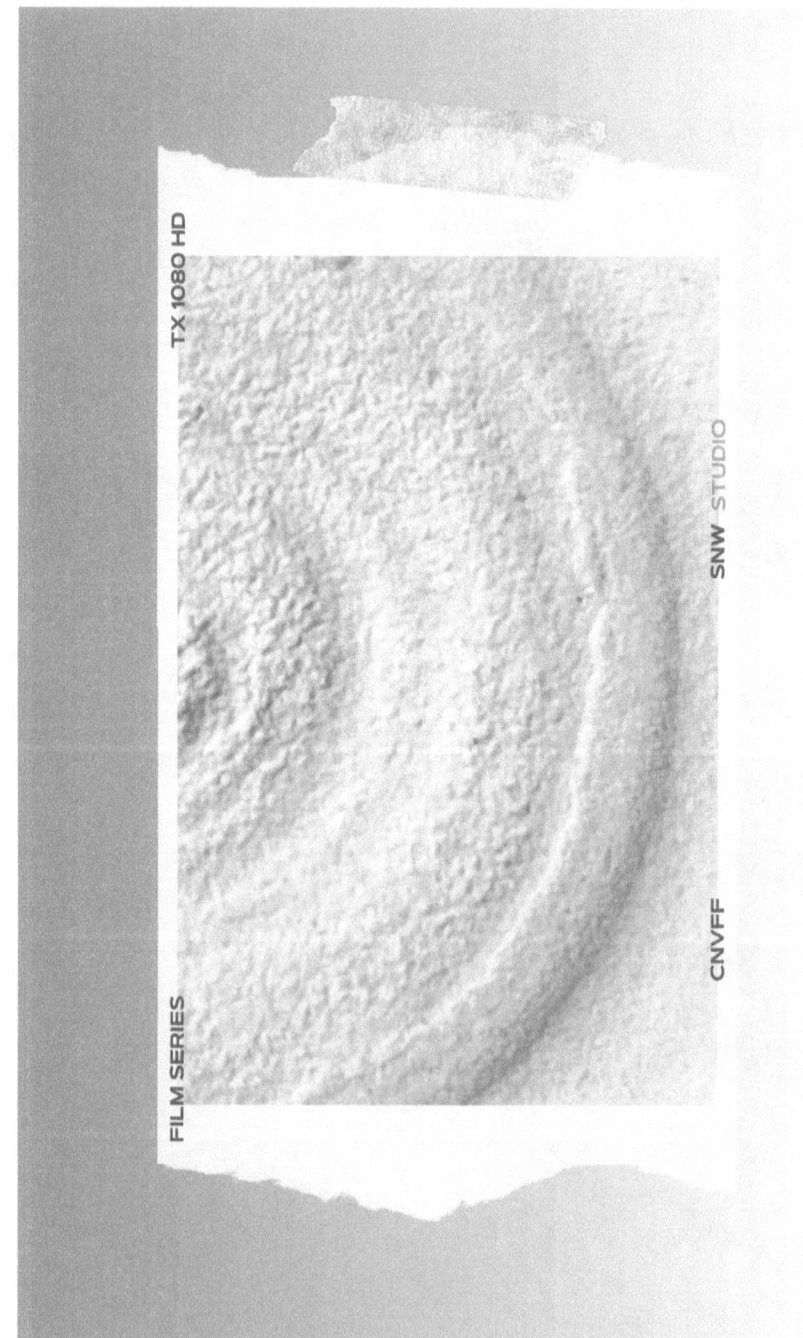

Tranquil Touch

Let me
Hold your
Brilliant
Mind
In these hands
And swirl
Those licks of
Tousled hair
To pull
Tension
From
Treacherous thoughts
The cues
Of your rhythm
Elicit ripples
From furrowed brows
And
Tense
Jaws
And pause
Let me bring you
To life
And rock you
To sleep
In these arms
That crave
Your release

Good Mourning

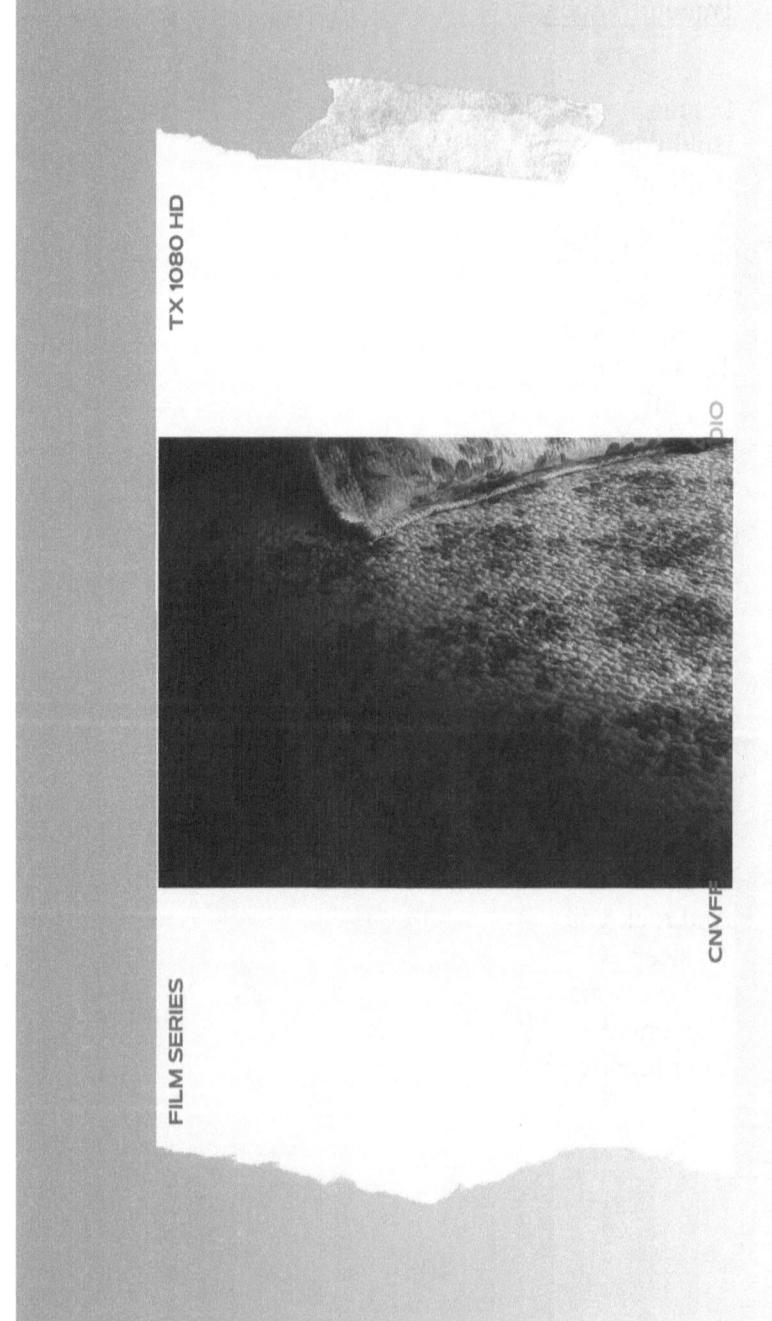

Layover

More than an afterthought
In the aftermath
Of words whispered
At 2am
Sleep displaced
As ease slips in
And asks for evening tea
To stay
The night
With
Me

Good Mourning

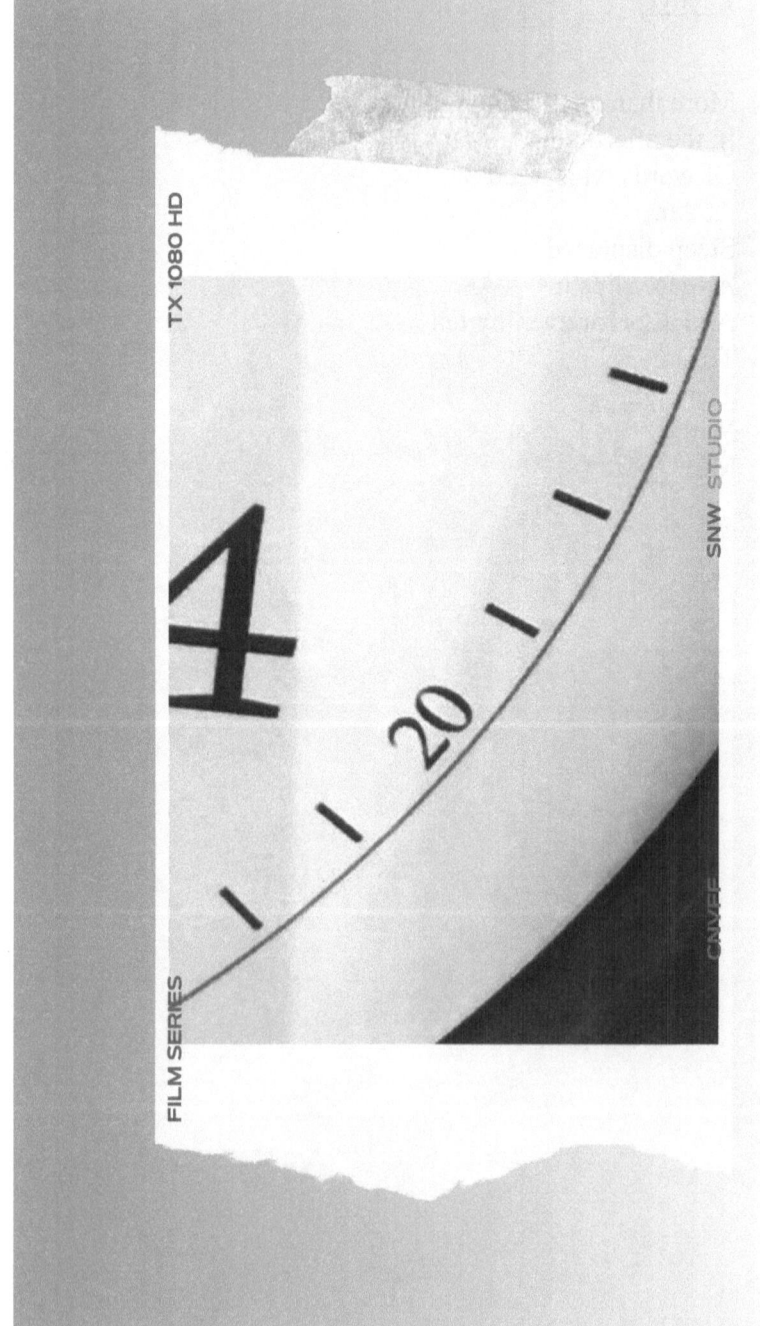

Lullaby

Been up so long
Circadian
Rhythm is long
Long gone
And all that plays
In the back of my mind is
Your song
Sing to me, love
Sing me to sleep like
The sheep
Can go home
And your tone
Calls me quiet
For a rest
Where the moon
Does her job
And the sun finally sets
Settle me in
Nestle me in
And lay out this
Sheet
Untangle the rope
For an untethered throat
To pass time
Where your time
Resides
As it should
By my side

Good Mourning

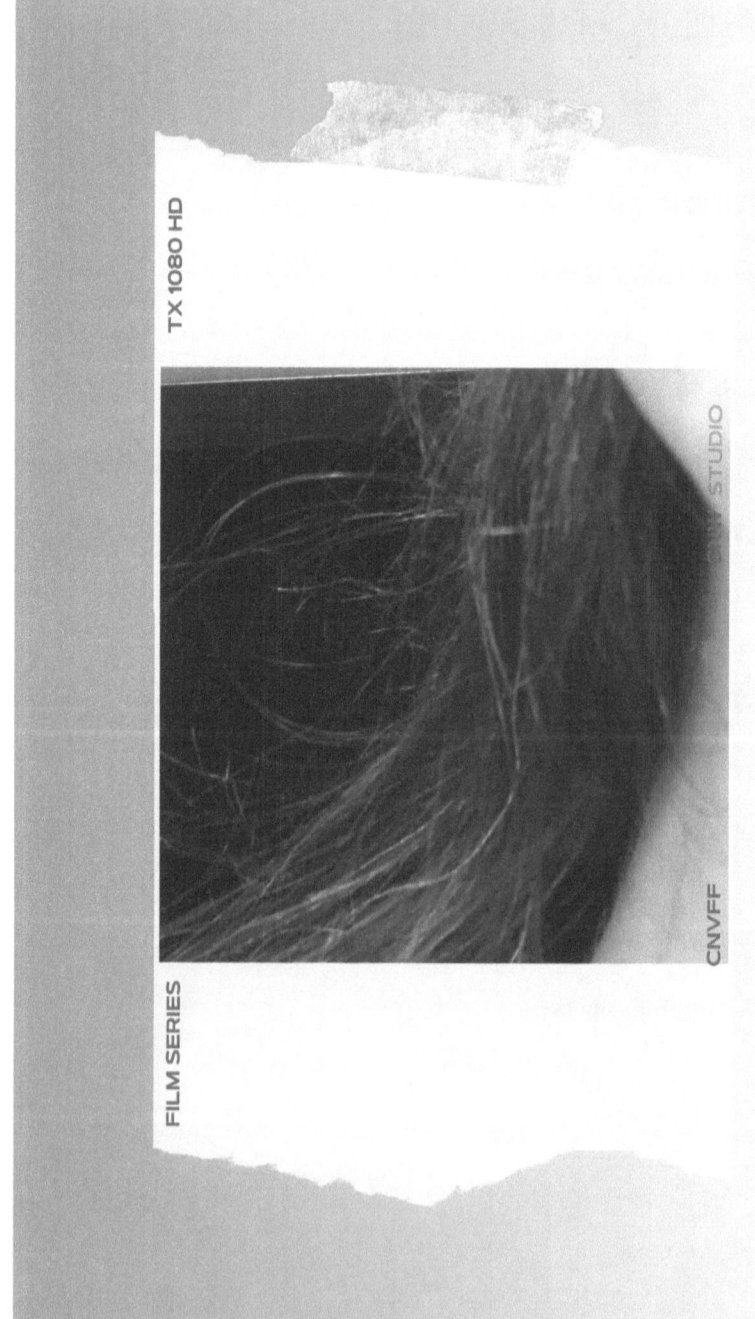

Supine and Prepared

All I could hear
Was
Wet velvet
Slipping its way
Into my ears
Down full length
Of spine
Supine and prepared
I could smell
His intention
And my essence
Became his playground
And we played
And played
And played

Soaked

Lavender laden
Steam
Drifts
To the heavens
And welcomes
Tired muscles
Wary from demands
Of stubborn life
Sink low
Into fragrant waters
Of peace
And stroke
My toes
One by one
Slipping a finger
Between
Resurfacing
Repeating
Replaying
Scenes in my memory
Of where those
Capable hands
Have been
Cupping curves
And tracing lengths
Of trembling
Ribs
Brought to life
By your
Energy

And expertise
To
See
Me

Good Mourning

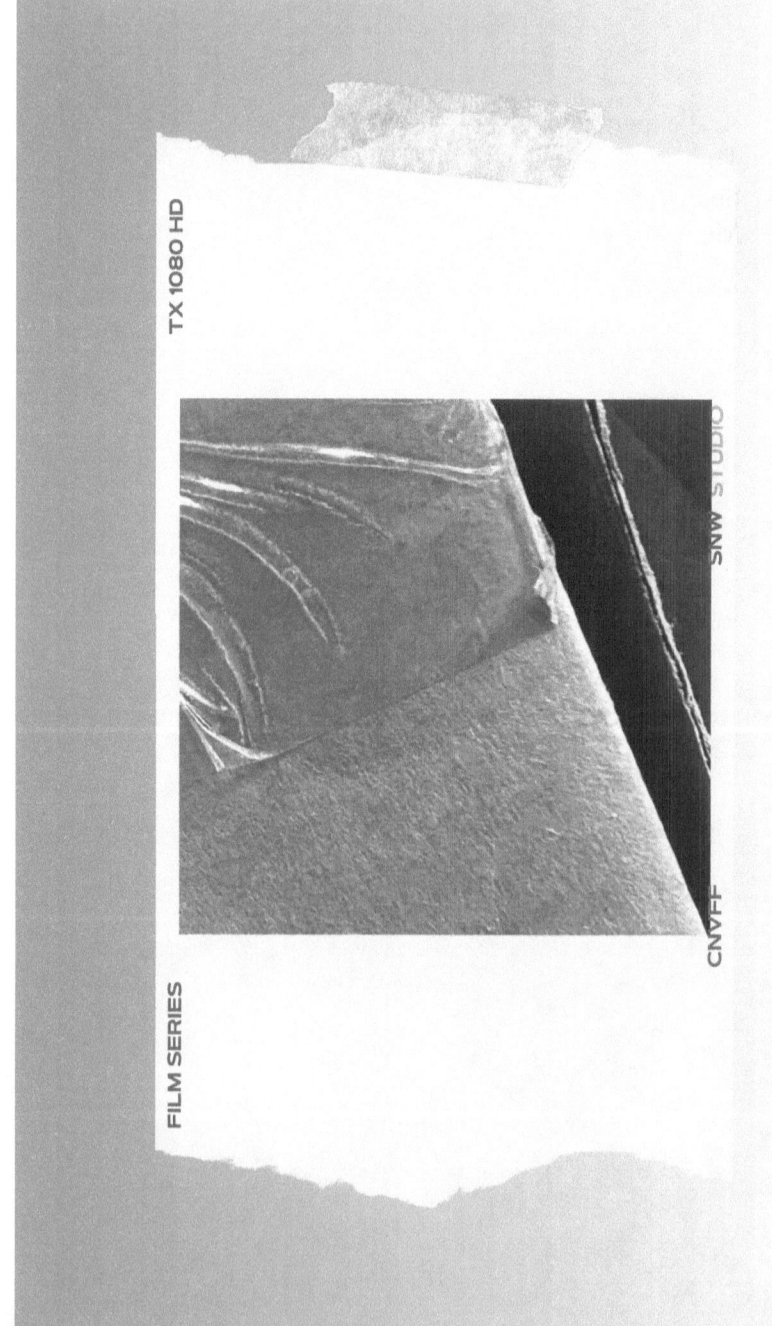

Innocence Disbarred

I gave it away
Before I knew
It was
Mine

Good Mourning

Flourish

Sunset words
Soft on lips
Like rain
Settled deep in
Cloud bellies
With plans we
Can smell
In the air
Crisp
Filled with tomorrow
In the works
But for tonight
Let's have tonight
And pour promises
From thirsty
Thoughts
To hungry
Hands
Let it rain
Let it rain
Let it rain
While tomorrow takes its time
And steps
Into view

Good Mourning

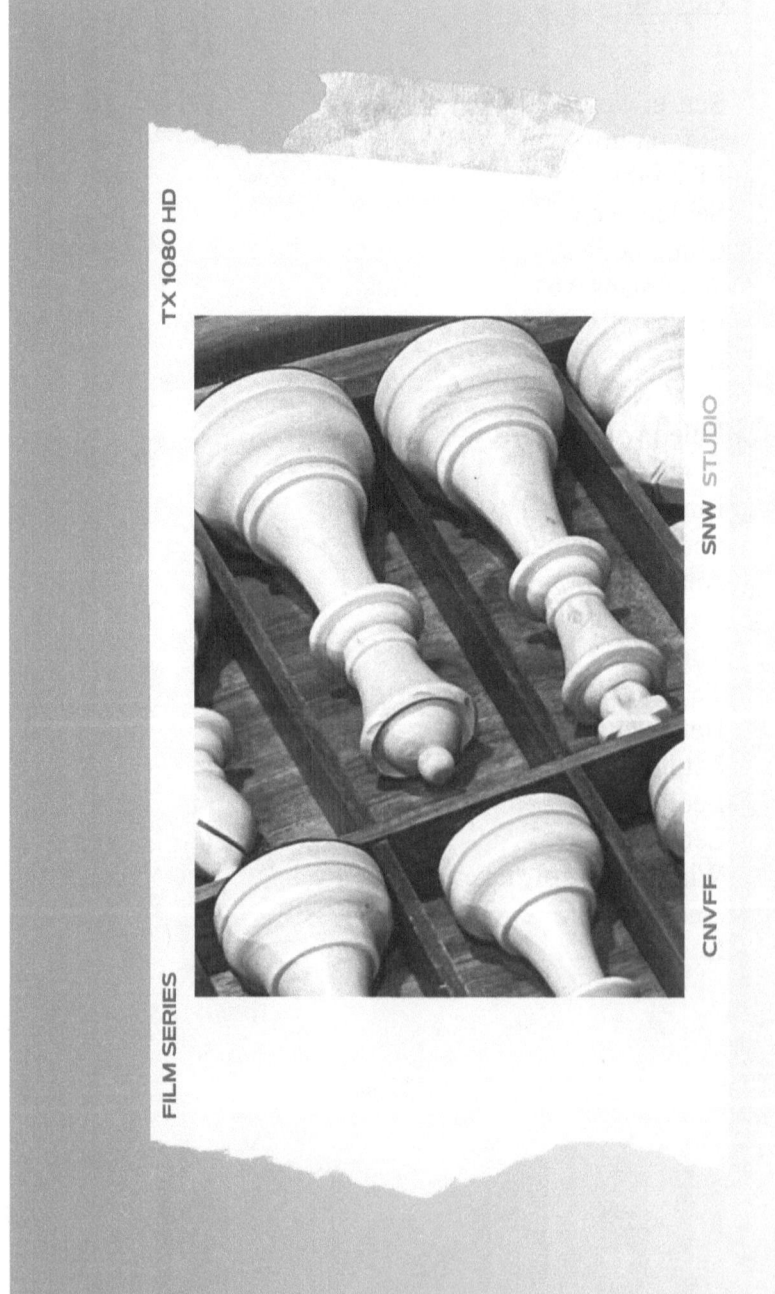

TX 1080 HD
SNW STUDIO
CNVFF
FILM SERIES

<u>Leave the Gate</u>
    <u>as you found it</u>

Tepid thoughts and lonely hands
Settle for seconds
While the main course
Is destined for
Eager list makers
And time takers
Calling us back
To the settled course of
A lure
Of forced entry
Where the deadbolt doesn't matter
When the gate
Is wide open
Floodgate of lessons, then
Lesson plans with plans
To generate
An itinerary with bulletproof alibies
And a towel
To wipe
The mess

Good Mourning

The Archives

He loves me like
A grand museum piece
With eyes wide
Awake and eager
Seeking
To interpret
Broad strokes
Of my
History
The solitary mystery
Of what is
Behind the glass
Pursing lips
That have never known
Home
Until slipping past
The velvet rope

Sanctuary

She stayed so long
Her sanctuary
Became
Her prison
With nothing left to do
But pace
The days to completion
With tired
Uninspired
Callouses
That begged her to
Swim
To run
To explore
Terrain that had not existed
Before
Before she built tall walls
To keep them out
And keep her safe
With promise
Of
Safekeeping
Like a diary of secrets
That no one
Held the key
To
To peek within
The pages of what once made her
Smile
Or gasp

Or yearn for more time
More time to
Live a life
Of safety
Unperturbed
Undisturbed
Until breath runs out
And bones
Are called to dust
With calloused feet
Worn thin
For safety
In her sanctuary
Of solitude

Good Mourning

Nibble

A lover knows
Quick release
Is a mere
Appetizer
A bite between
But the feast
Is in
The
Pace

Sanctity

So tell me, you love me
And shout it with
Full lungs
Filled with childlike glee
With arms wrapped firm
Around my waist
As pools of love
Fill your gaze
Whisper, careful
Like it's a secret
Like it's the secret
To life
To breath
To it all
Place my chin
In
The palm of your hand
And pet my hair
As lips brush
Tender thoughts
Between curious eyes
And you draw the bath
To soak my feet
With promise of a lifelong feast
That awaits
Love me fiercely
Love me unabashed
Unrestricted
Under oath
Of the declaration you gift me

Brenda Baker

The gift
Of your heart
With a seat for two
At the table
We built
With our own hands

Good Mourning

Seascapes and Scandal

Eyes are soft
And evenings
Laid to
Rest
Like your back
Against my
Belly
Breathing memories
Encapsulated
Emancipated
With pulse
Of an ocean floor
Full of life
And stories
Reserved for deep dive
Exploration
And time to
Taste the bait

Good Mourning

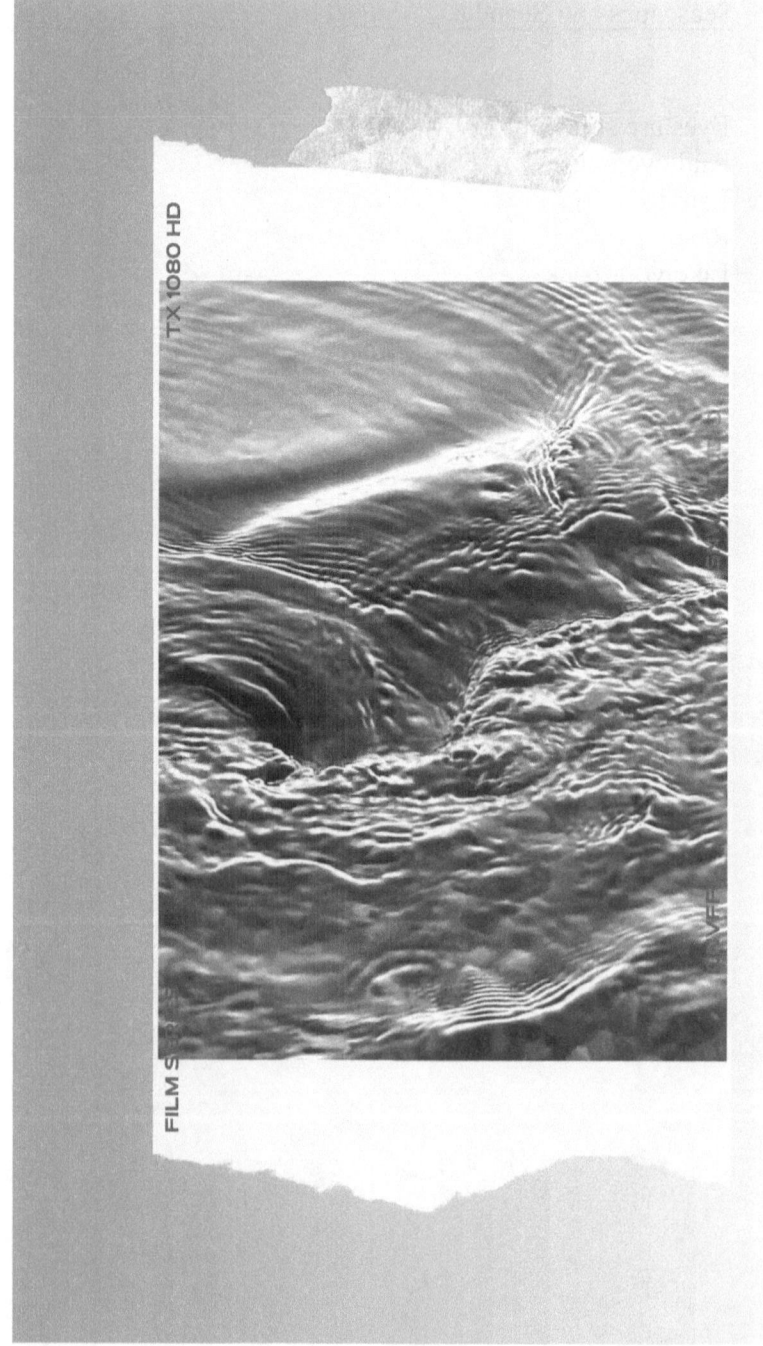

Reclamation Place

He had never touched
Something
So wild

Good Mourning

Evening Envelopes

It's a somber
Strange thing
To love you hard
And release
You
Soft
Into the night

Good Mourning

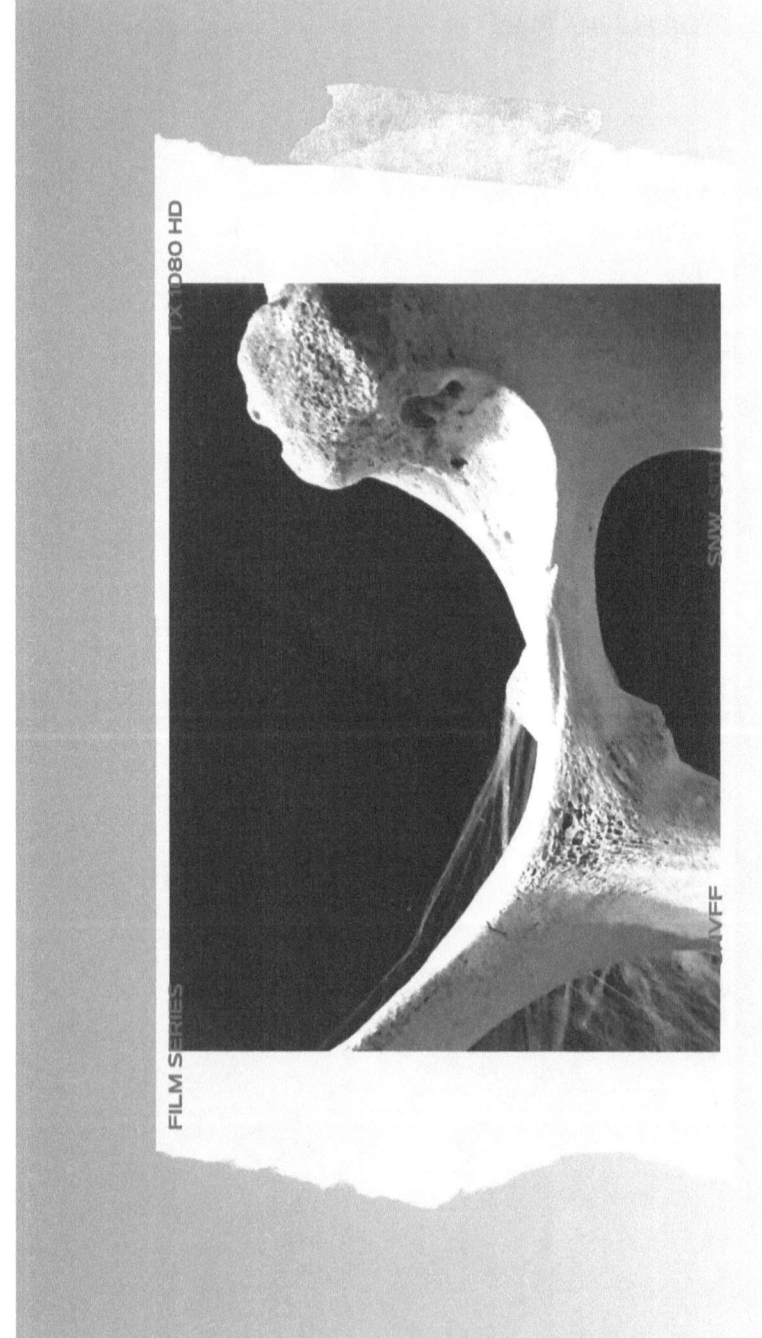

'Til Death Do Us Part

An alchemist
Approach
To slide of hand
That locks in
First kisses in
The morning
And hands to hold
As the threat of
Everything old
Creeps in
And spreads us all
To dust

Good Mourning

Linger

I belong
In the long
Sweet moments
Before
Sun sneaks in
And rouses you from
Slumber
Remember
Me
Between sleepy arms
With slow
Beat
And lips that
Kiss the day to start
Let's start
Careful then
And begin
Again
And again
And again once more

Good Mourning

An Inside Inquisition

It wasn't a self-love
Deficiency
It was a miseducation
Of the representation
That left me
Placid
And raw
To infection of an affliction
That held me
Motionless
With feet stitched
To shoes
That didn't fit

Good Mourning

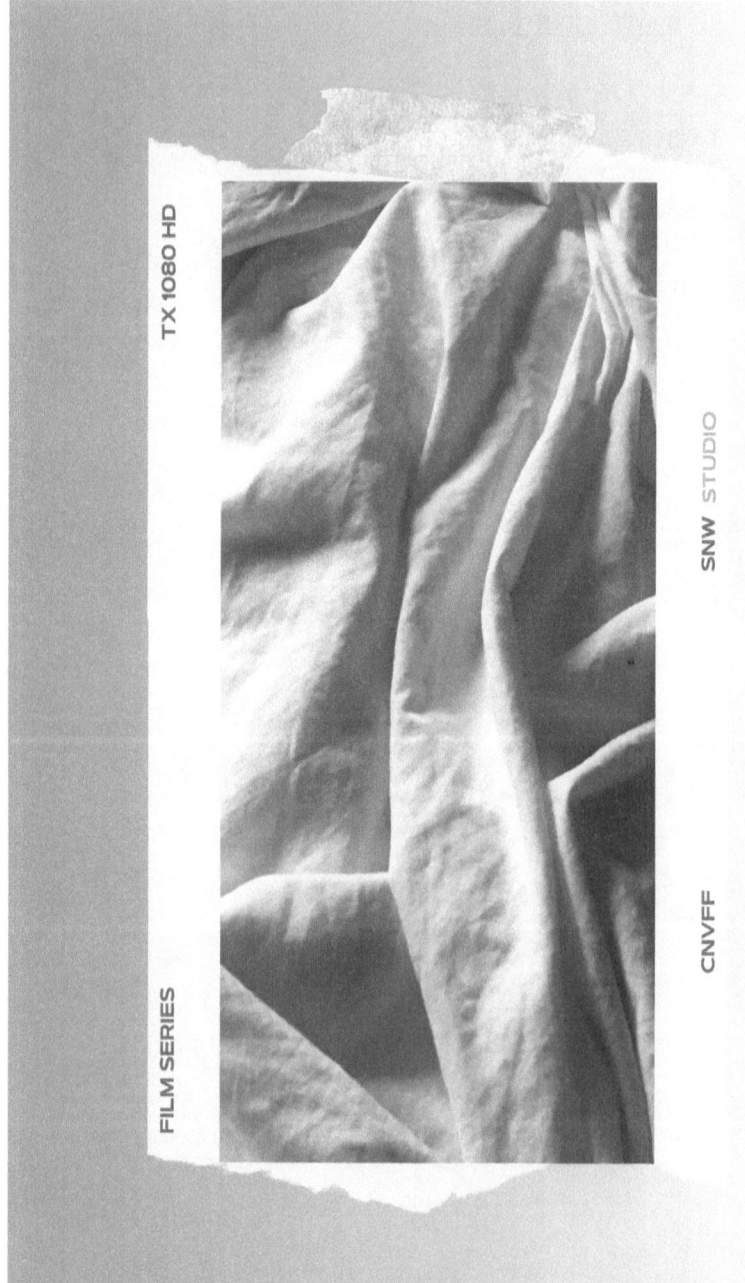

Knitting Strings

Simplify
My busy mind
And search the sky
For sun
Another day
Has parted ways
Before it has begun
But in this cast
Of broken bone
A gentle whisper
Calls for home
And noodle soup
To soothe the soul
With blankets warmed
By love alone

The Storm

Face down
With ankles crossed
Instructed to
Wait
Arms above
Palms pressed
In pause
In prayer
Gratitude
For your appetite
And
How you play
I will wait
Still
So still
As hands mark
Their journey
Traipsing impatient curvature
And trembling skin
As pressure swells
Indicating
This is more than
Just
Good fun
This feeds the soul
Bite by bite
Leaning close to fully
Inhale
What you've created
My heat

Radiates
And you
Assert
Your position

Good Mourning

Tuesdays

Caution is tossed
Aside
With reckless beat
Jackets
And shoes
Follow suit
As lights fade
And hands become
Nightlights
To guide
Soft secure spaces
Intended for touch
That only
Tells time
In hours
And lifetimes

Good Mourning

A Deliberate Devotion

Fade in gently
With curling tendrils
Of your power in my palm
Pacified by embrace
Cradled in the crook of my arm
With skin meant for
Whispers and murmurs
Tongue trapsing
Skin smooth
Prepared just for you
Dipping deep in pools of
Effort
That gather in the
Collarbone
And less obvious locations
As destinations
Settle down to a midnight pace
Rising and resting
With the tides
Of inside

Good Mourning

Template to Contemplate

If smiles hold secrets
And memories hold
Sweet dips of passion
Moments meant
For your touch
And my feel
Then let it stretch
From ear to ear
While messing about
With the
Tedious bits of life
That dreams
Of the soft pulse of your mouth
And carries on
By thoughts
Of you

Good Mourning

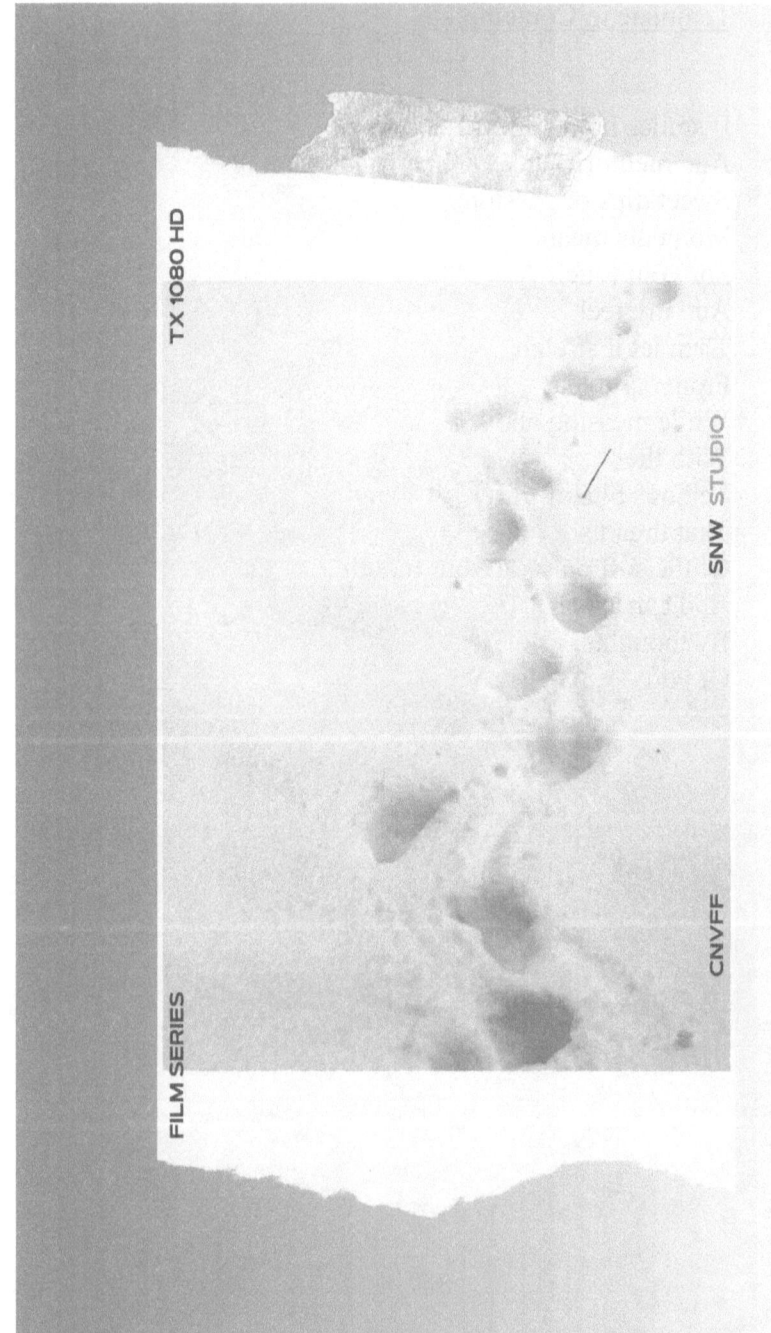

Tracks

Make no mistake
If you track me
I will
Let you find me
I will
Invite you to tea
I will
Let you in
And watch the life
Drain from your eyes
As you become victorious
And realize
You've hunted a hunter

Limitless

I touch my skin
Letting eyelids
Rest
All the way closed
My mind's eye
Will do the seeing
This evening
As compass hands
Encompass subtle
Viscosity of water
And unexpected delight
Of my own
Fingertips
Along length of smooth thighs
A cadence slow
Roaming tempo
That demands nothing of me
But to listen
To feel
The pull of
Pressure I crave
Locations call to me
All of them mine
For exploring
For enjoying
And I tell this world to wait
I will not have walked
This
Earth
Inside this skin

For all eternity
And not know her well
With ears to soul
And palms to place
I listen closely
To maps
Of
Limits that do not
Exist

Good Mourning

Canvas

The rolling of you
In me
Inside
My mind's eye
Elicits unfamiliar desire
To just receive
Let it simmer
As collections
Of memories
Of spices
Of long-distance endurance
Fueled by your North arrow
Strength and desire
To please
And be pleased
Pull me in
And it is alluring
You leave much to be
Imagined
And my imagination is vast
Filled with every color you'd
Choose
To use
And paint my skies

Good Mourning

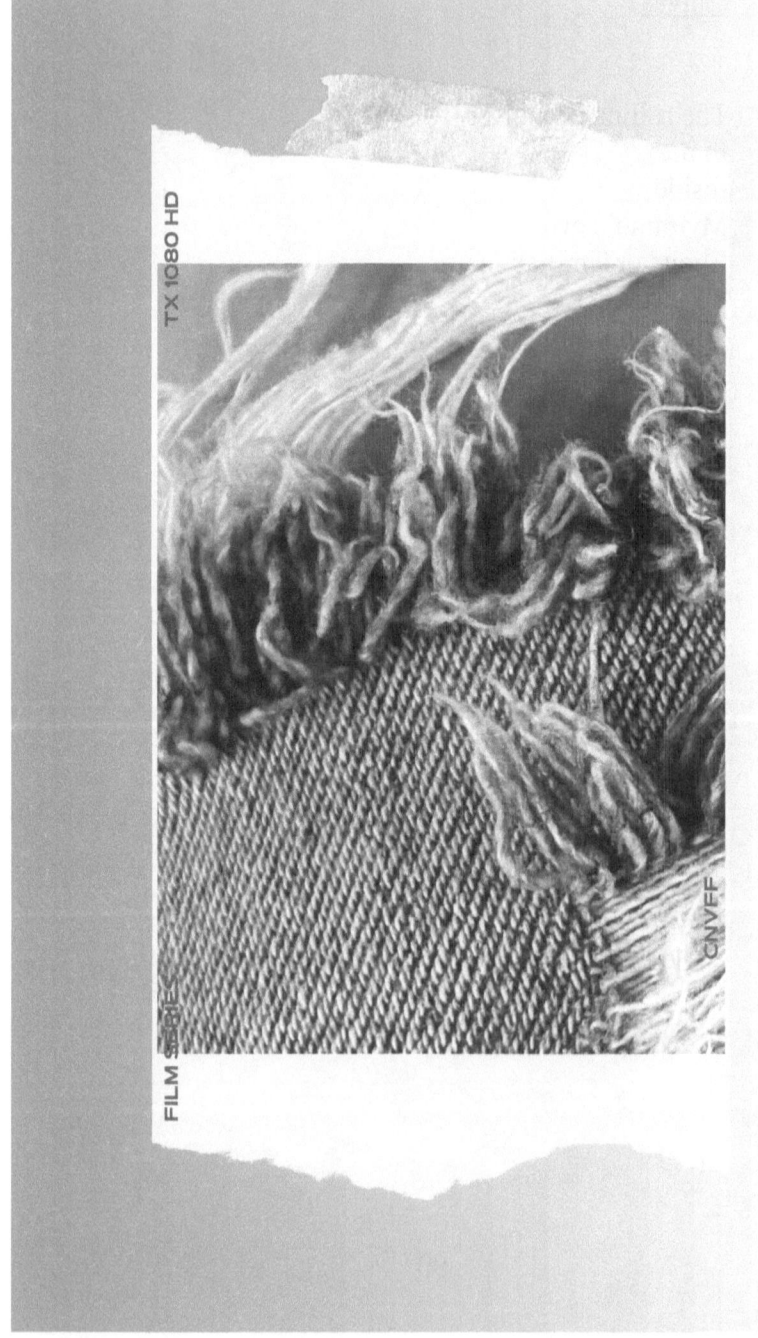

Abide

There is such pleasure
In the texture
Of what lingers
Where you've kissed
This skin
That beckons
You
Your scent
Entangled in mine
Such a fine
New fragrance
It speaks of
Travels to be taken
Of
Memories to remember
Of mornings
Where you know how
I like it slow
And I know how
You like
My tempo
How you like me
Skin to skin
And
Positioned just so

Good Mourning

The Builder

A casual composted
Conspiracy
Of love notes
Love you so
Little castings
Cast aside
To make room
For the cream
Within
A symphony siphons
Solitude
And
Solid floors splinter
Toothpicks
To pluck
The remnants
That remain
After the rain

Good Mourning

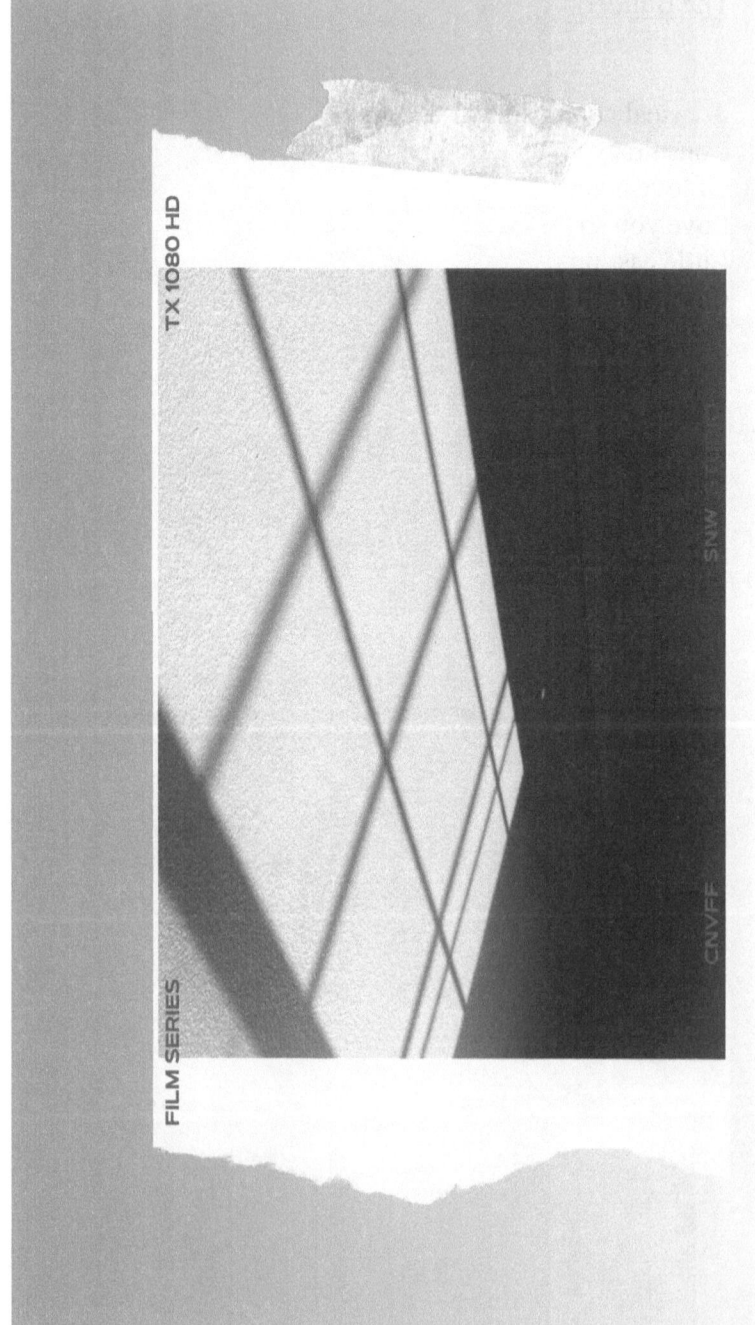

Promenade for Two

I will devour
His appetite
For my touch
Between
My lips
And his smile
And our story
Unfolding
Silent
Onlookers drawn
To watch this display
Parade and sway
Past
Their tepid
Conversations
Our heat
Radiates
Rotates
Heads
But my sights are set
On the strength
In his
Hands
The want
In his
Gaze
As feet sit still
And erupt into flames

Present

Limbs draped casually
Resting solid on bare skin
As if it were
Never
A
Question
Of possession
And expression
Just peace
And time
Love and breath
As fingertips
Draw liminal
Circles
Slow and without
Purpose
Nonchalant and
Casual
Casting
Cascading sparks
That spread from hip to thigh
To heart and thoughts
Of how those
Fingers
Taste
In heated moments
Where bodies become
Vessels
Of wordless conversation
And I taste

Brenda Baker

You
And me
Wrapped together
As one
In a perfect package
Delivered
Directly to
The back of
My throat

Good Mourning

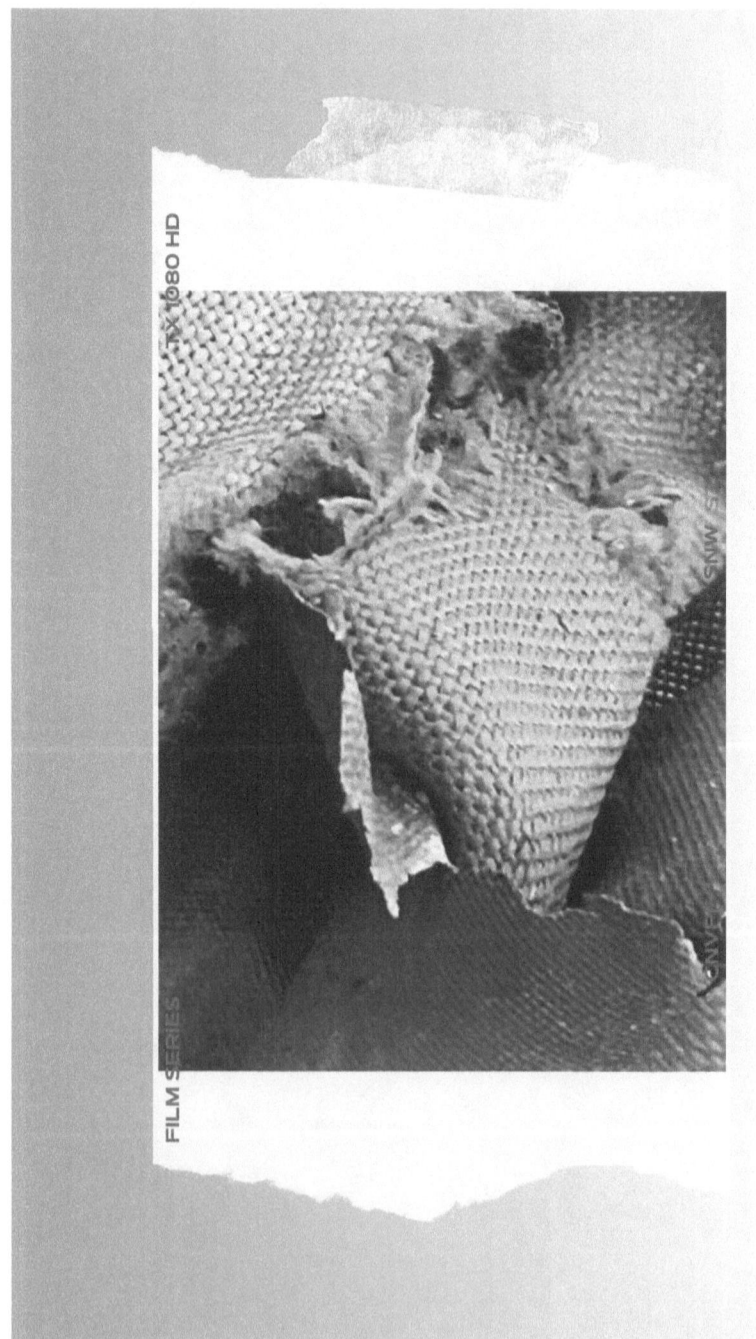

Tender Topography

Settle down
Slow
And easy then
Into these arms
That have called to you
Through sleepless evenings
And insatiable
Hunger
Relieved only
By the energy
Of your love
Roll into my embrace
Gently then
As shoulders relax
And breath meets time
And home
Eyes seeking nothing
Anymore
Only receiving
While fingertips
Paint maps
Of territories
Undisclosed

Good Mourning

Refuse

I refuse
Resist
Reset
This prison of
A wary mind
Where your words once
Dictated and
Directed
How I got to breathe
And why I wasn't worth it
Anyway
Because these days
The sun shines
Despite
Words encased in malice
And the birds sing
Despite
Inner
Tormented
Terrors
Of fears that
No longer exist
And the wind whispers
A lullaby of
Choice
To choose
What can partake
And what I take
Away
Like curbside
Trash

So, Stay

Squandered beads of sweat
Perch the arch
Of cautious brows
With heavy breaths
Labored by
An inky sky
Rendezvous
That somehow
Sidestepped
An evening adieu
How do
These next steps go
Then
If the curious sun
With crimson shades
Draws the shades
And shines on what's anew
While daybreak
Slips into view
In tiny
Cracks
Between
Me and you?
Coffee then
Is next for us
As we explore
More
Than either of us
Planned
For

For lips met dreams
With sleep delayed
That felt like
Memories
Still to come
As hands held
And healed
And called us both
Here

Good Mourning

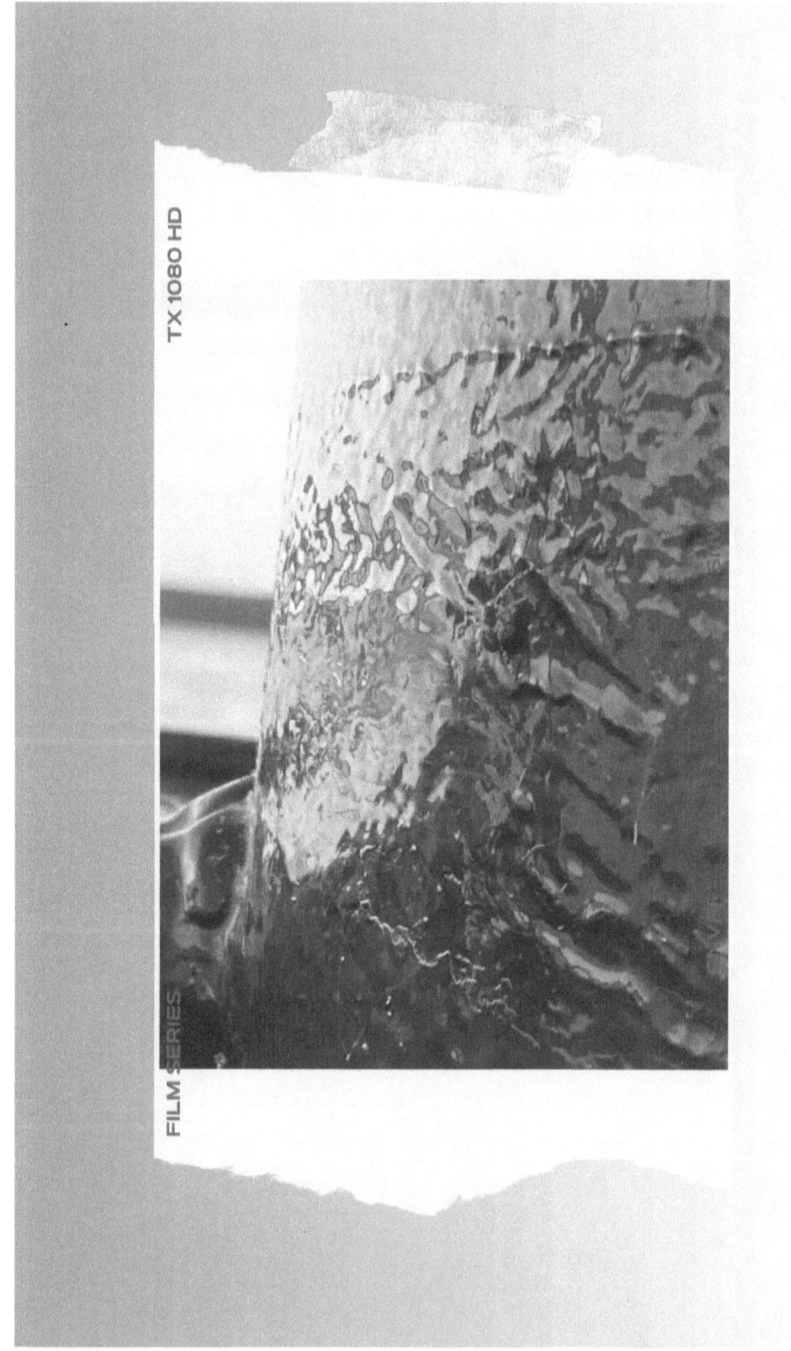

Twilight Stroll

Take your time
As the chorus
Between
Us
Closes in
And breath
Fuses to intention
An electricity
Within
That awakens
Us
To stroll along
Forgotten avenues
Where we wander
Soft lit streets
Like lovers
With hands intertwined
And destiny
Yet to be determined

Good Mourning

Reservations

I've come back
Three times now
To an empty seat
That sways
With careful
Cautious
Calloused
Sorrow
Why did you paint the sky
With promises
To my eager eyes
Just
To curtly curl
A sideways glare
And watch words wilt
Like daisies plucked
And left
To fade
In a jar
On the side of
This solitary table
With placemats for two
And echoes of
Only one

Good Mourning

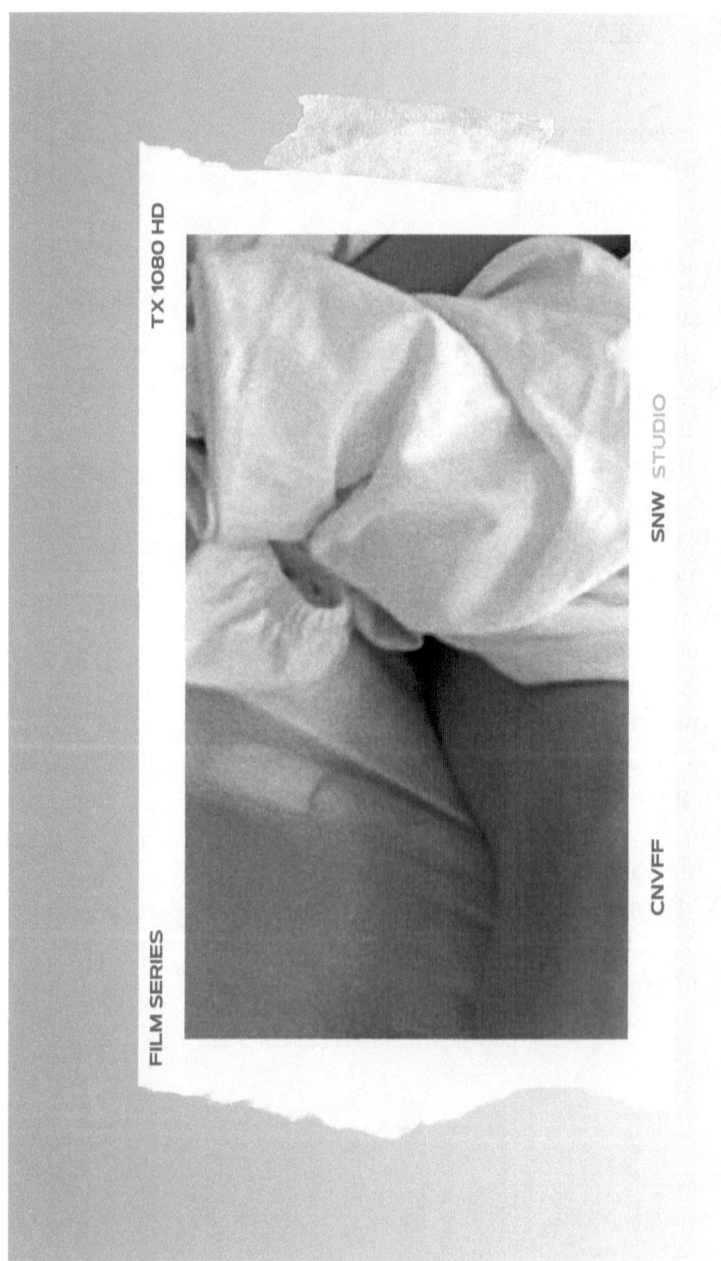

Lust and Line

Legs entangled
Casually draped across
Linens that
Know too much

Good Mourning

Apex Trance

Sunlight sly
Capsized by
A wanton, sallow
Naked eye
Coursing strings
Cascading things
As rivers pass us by
A symphony
Cacophony
Of wishes prayed
Remain unmade
And summon time
Come true
Will you, please
Be ever pleased
With moon drop lips
And starlight seeds
To reap
And sow
And plant the things
To bring
Us back
To life

Good Mourning

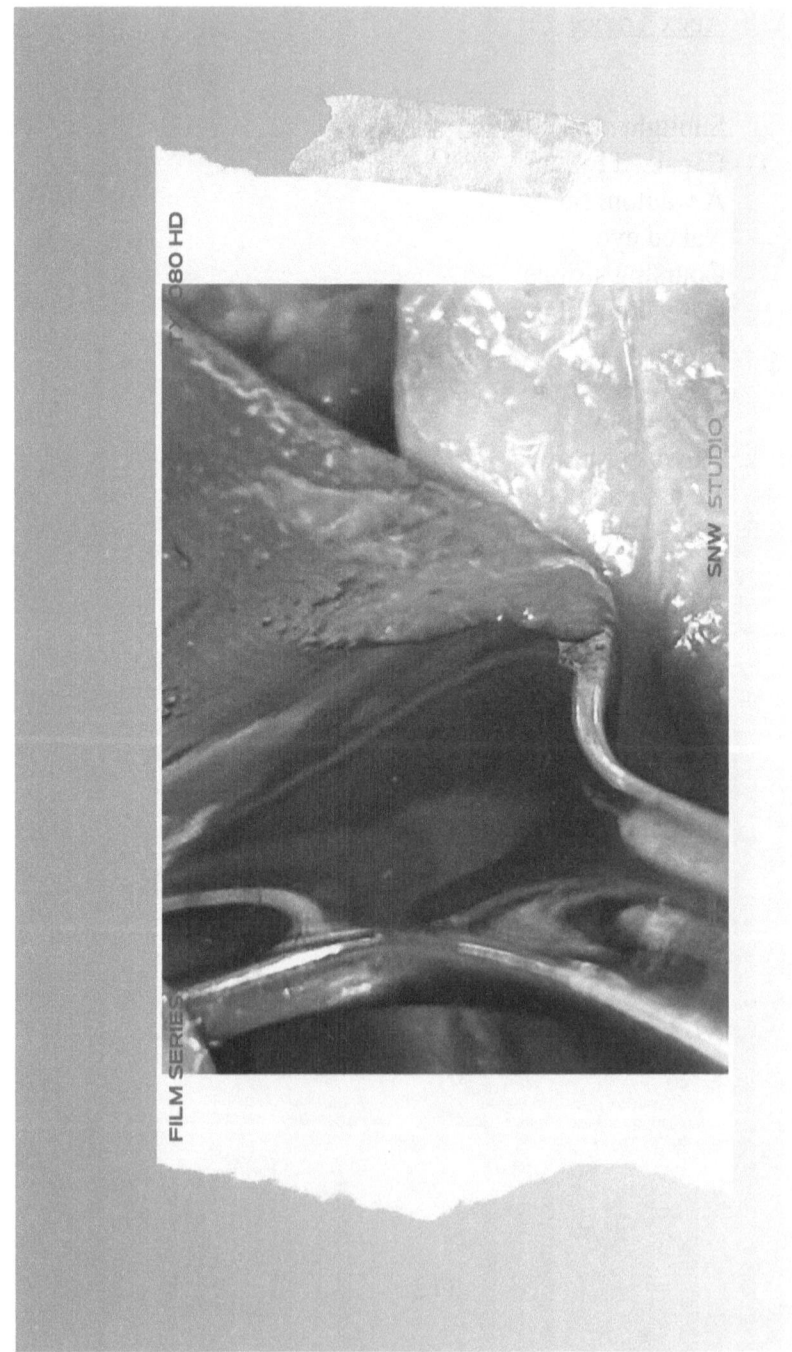

Carnal Cuisine

This love
Is a new
Category
Of consumption

Good Mourning

Leap

Cavernous cravings
Lift us to the
Lip of the edge
And tempt
Us heartily
Jump, then
Jump to your end and
End this
Effortless
Evasive
Enigma
Of curiosity
That only settles with
A thorough petting
Not putting off
The
Task of highest
Priority
Of you under me

Good Mourning

An Evening's Pass

Isn't the longing
A bit exquisite?
Anticipation in the ache
When reprieve
Is waiting in the wings
A subdued
And not subtle
Discomfort
Let it ride, then
Ride 'til dawn
And sleep by the shrubbery
In waiting
For sunbeams to sing
A new day is here
For the taking
Take her
Softly then
In palms of safety
And wrap fingers
Right around
That delicate heart
To whisper
"I've brought us flowers, love."

Good Mourning

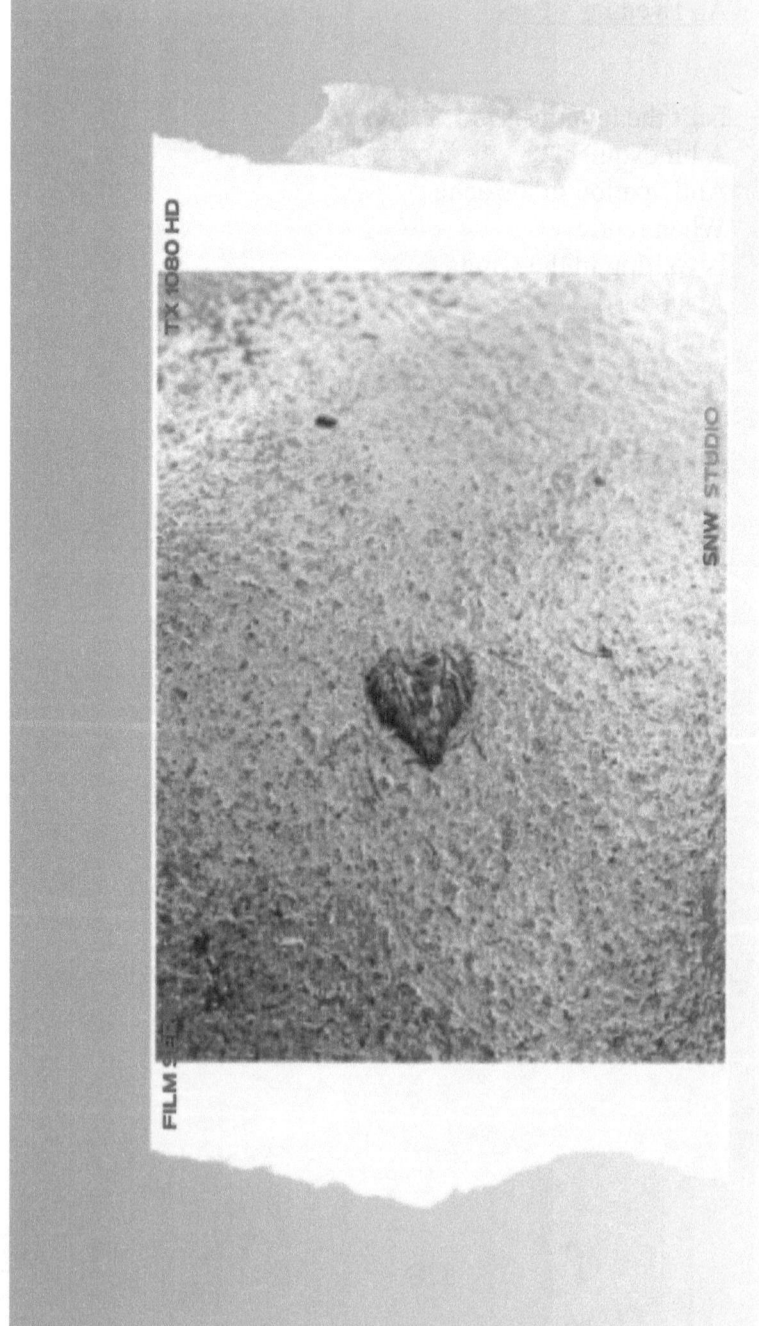

All the Way Down

Handfuls of you
Firm grip
After grasp
Beads of
Sweat
Become
Oceans of liquid
Promise
As I sample
Your secrets
And swallow
Them whole

Good Mourning

Last Supper

Furrowed brows set
The table
And nothing is left
To eat
Our bones, once thick with marrow
Sit quiet
In the chairs that were
Homes of laughter
Visions of future plans
Scatter themselves far flung
So as not to
Burn
In the flames of
Spark between eyes
That used to set passion in motion
Now dry
And cracked from tears that fill canyons
Bent on
Making it out
Alive

Good Mourning

Soothe

Place tender hands
On weathered skin
That
Learned the hard way
Love
Can soothe the
Canyons
Crafted by
Wishes unfulfilled
And a timeline
Turned to
Frayed edges and
Smoke
As fingers trace
Where a smile used
To play
The warmth of
Possibilities
Creep back into view
And sunsets
Have new meaning

Breathe

She took a lover
An unforeseen sidestep
Directly into the
Pathway
Of warmed oil and play
It was all new
The whole thing
Yet her body knew this dance
As if it had been
The sole focus
Of a multi-year
Study abroad program
His hands held her reception
And she was awash
In options
Who could she be
In a place of such pleasure
And tension?
Common words
Would
Forever trigger memories
That engulf her inner galaxies
It would be her idea box
Her place of reference
When inspiration of daily tasks
Left her sallow
And cold
Warm summer nights
Bonfires
Options

Watching soft words roll
From his lips
Opened new dimensions within
Her
And she could finally
Breathe

Good Mourning

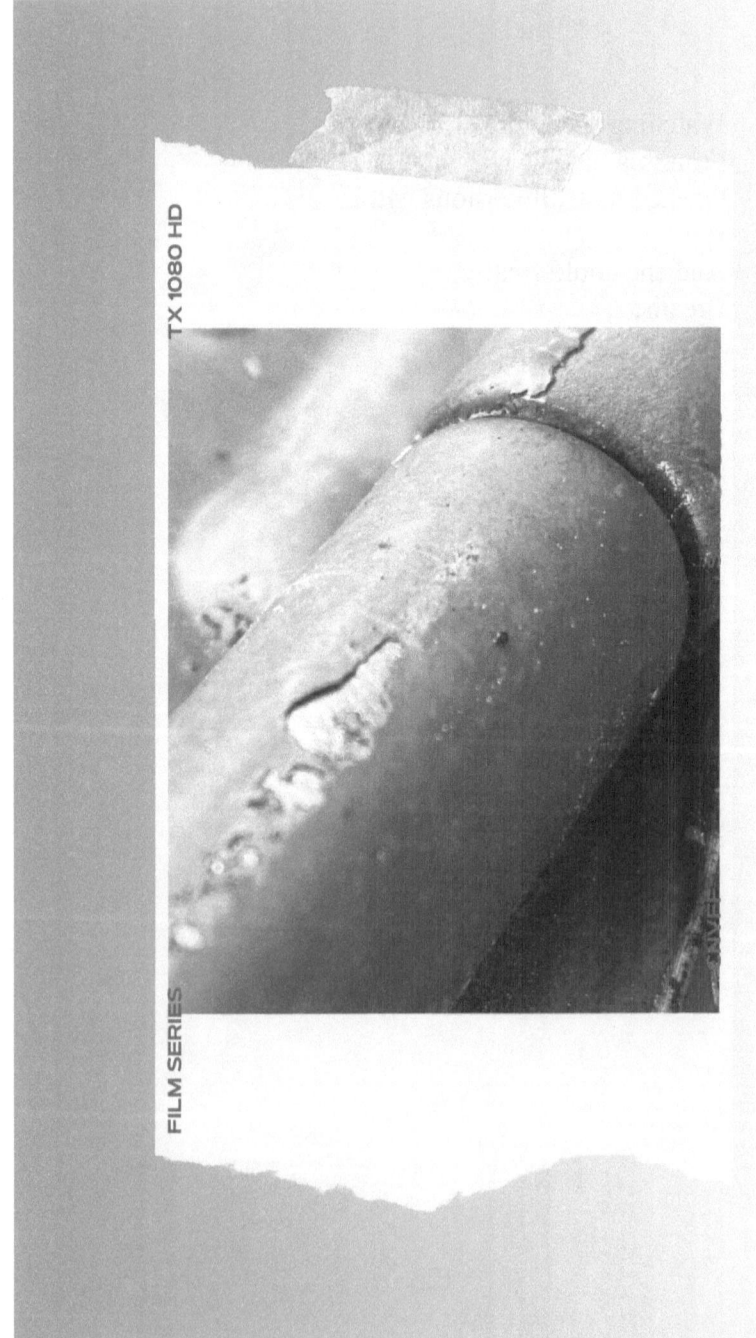

Radar

Your body beckons
And I hear
Your frequency
Frequently
As you plan
The slowest split
Between my legs

Good Mourning

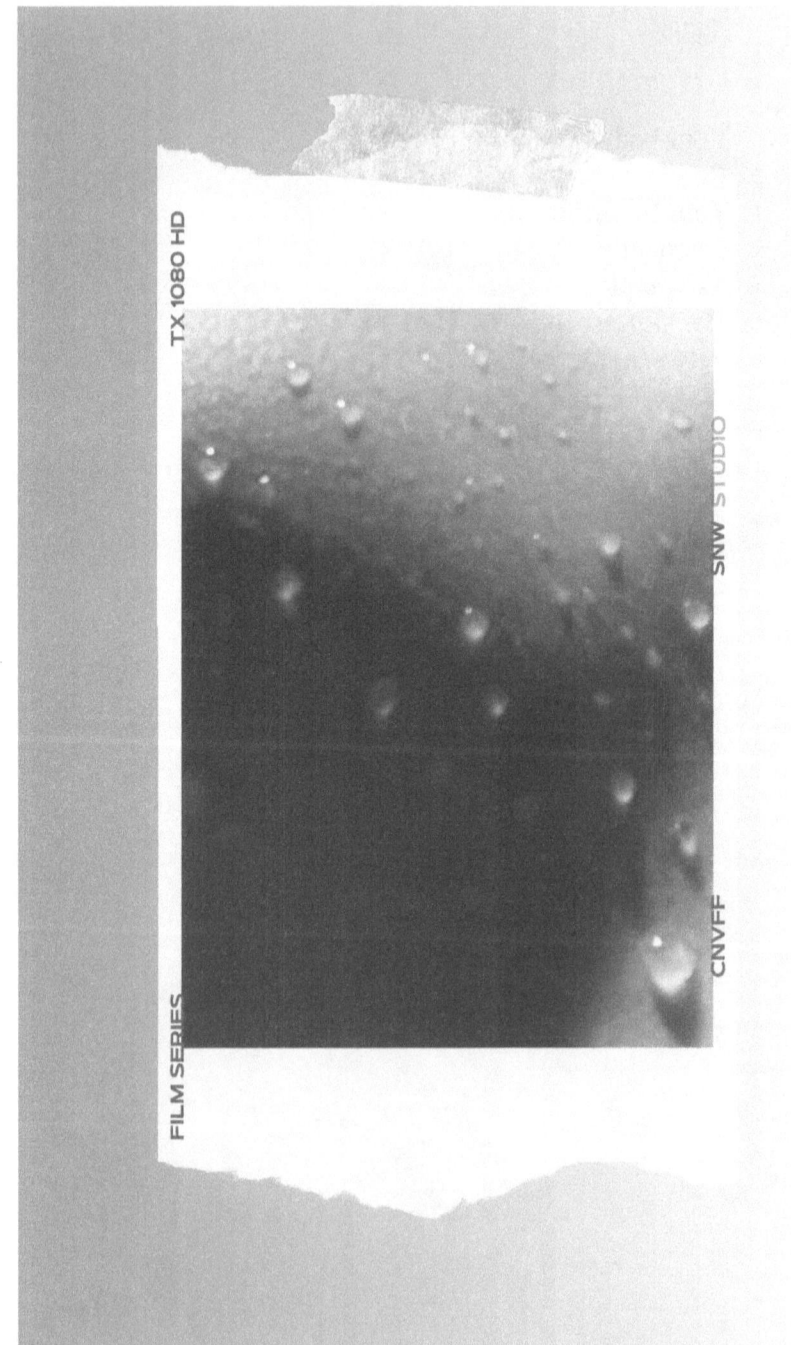

Supper Club

Patience has run its course
As footprints
Leave no trace
Of trails
Of trials
Of miles of pursuit
Wiped clean
In the wake
Of this suppertime
Frolic

Good Mourning

Yoga Tempo

Savasana
Rolls from your lips
With enduring peace
And pace
Of tongue
That knows language
Is just another form
Of connection
Like prolonged eye contact
Like sharing a meal
Made by hands of love
And intention
That pulls you back
Into the arms of
Memories
And whispers to your
Marrow
"All is well."
It's a still pose
For receiving
And my legs part slightly
Enough for me to know
And you to feel
The shift

Good Mourning

<u>Pursue; in due time</u>

She would be no match
For the patience
He possessed
To wait
Motionless
While she would roll herself
Onto her back
And ask trivial
Things
To fill the time
Until the inevitable
Nothing filled her
Anymore
For a new void
Had become
Excruciatingly present
Foreboding sleep
Dismissing ambient temperature
Calling to her
Attention
That nothing else will do
To a man
Such as this
30 days is nothing
Months are nothing
A slow blink
In the abundance
Of life
A slight pause
To bring

A humble approach
To breath itself
He will wait
As she will create
Sonnets
Of passion
Unveiling permission
To dip their toes
In the ripples
Of the river
Of life

Good Mourning

The Morning Always Comes

I will not lament
That I cannot keep the sunset

Good Mourning

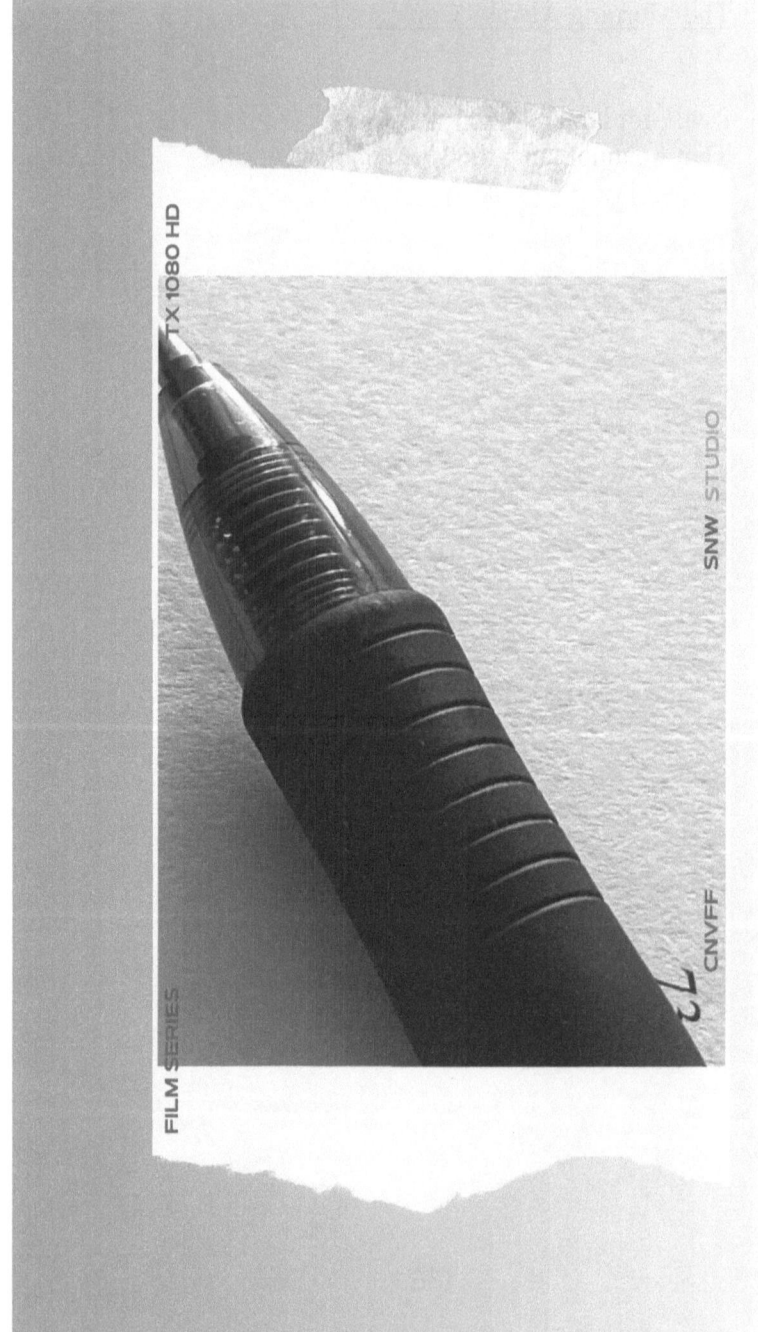

Noun of Safety

In soft early twilight
She'll slip from sheets
Where you tucked her in
To feel her naked feet
On cold tile
As stories
Tell her
How to move
That pen
And then
You'll see her sway
Stay silent
In these quiet moments
And watch the
Between worlds
Sing
That no one is privy to
But you
She can create near you
She can breathe near you
She lets her hair down
Puts her guard down
Sets her cup down
Overflowed by the freedom
To feel
In the safety
Of your love

Good Mourning

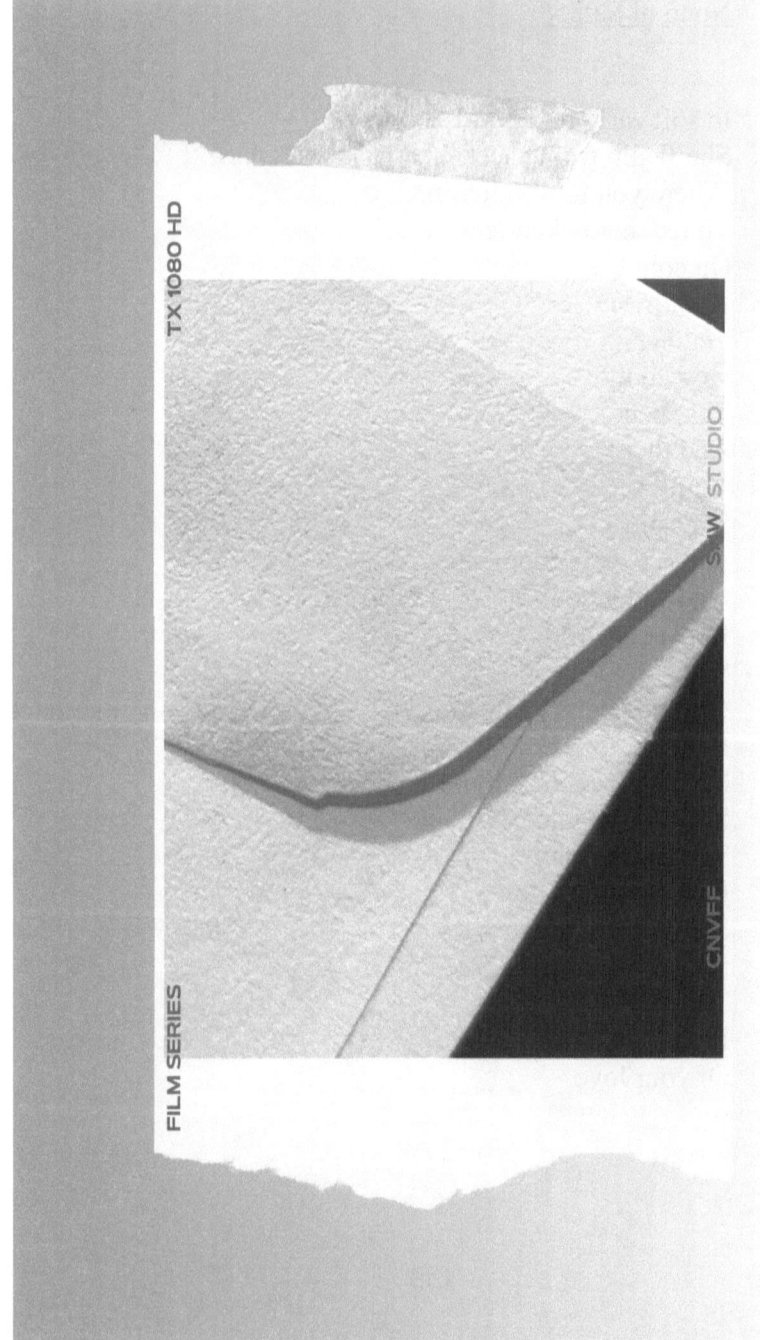

Thank You Notes

Sit me down with
Intention to pursue
The caverns of my heart
While
We sip casual coffee
On a balcony
Lush with life
We grow together
Time slows for our
Mornings
Laced with love
As you brush a
Knowing finger
Across my cheek
And whisper
To the sky

The Permission of Watermelon

Let me prepare it for you
The rind is
Sliced
In slow, long strips
And they slide
Aside
Revealing bright pink flesh
For devouring
With eyes locked
Yours on mine
Mine on yours
Sticky juices holding
Promises of thoughts
To come
And fingers slip
Piece after piece
Between the lips
And down the throat
Where words catch themselves
And hold restraint
Tight
As I imagine your hands
Would hold my wrists
Above me
Slip your fingers
Into my mouth
With a pace that
Pulls me to edge
Slow
So slow

Eyes locked on mine
My eyes to yours
As grips grasp tighter
The fruit
An afternoon selection
Becomes a gateway
Escape way
To feed more than
Empty bellies

Good Mourning

On Delay

Lips part slightly
As eyes
Sharpen
Their agenda
And I am your
Target
Patience
Pays off
As I accept my fate
And you
Slip inside
The warmth
Created by you
That delay
Now postponed
As our playful rendezvous
Skips gleefully
Across my mind
Through all hours
All moments
While time
Has been relieved
Of all duties
And now
All that remains
Is
To
Eat

Good Mourning

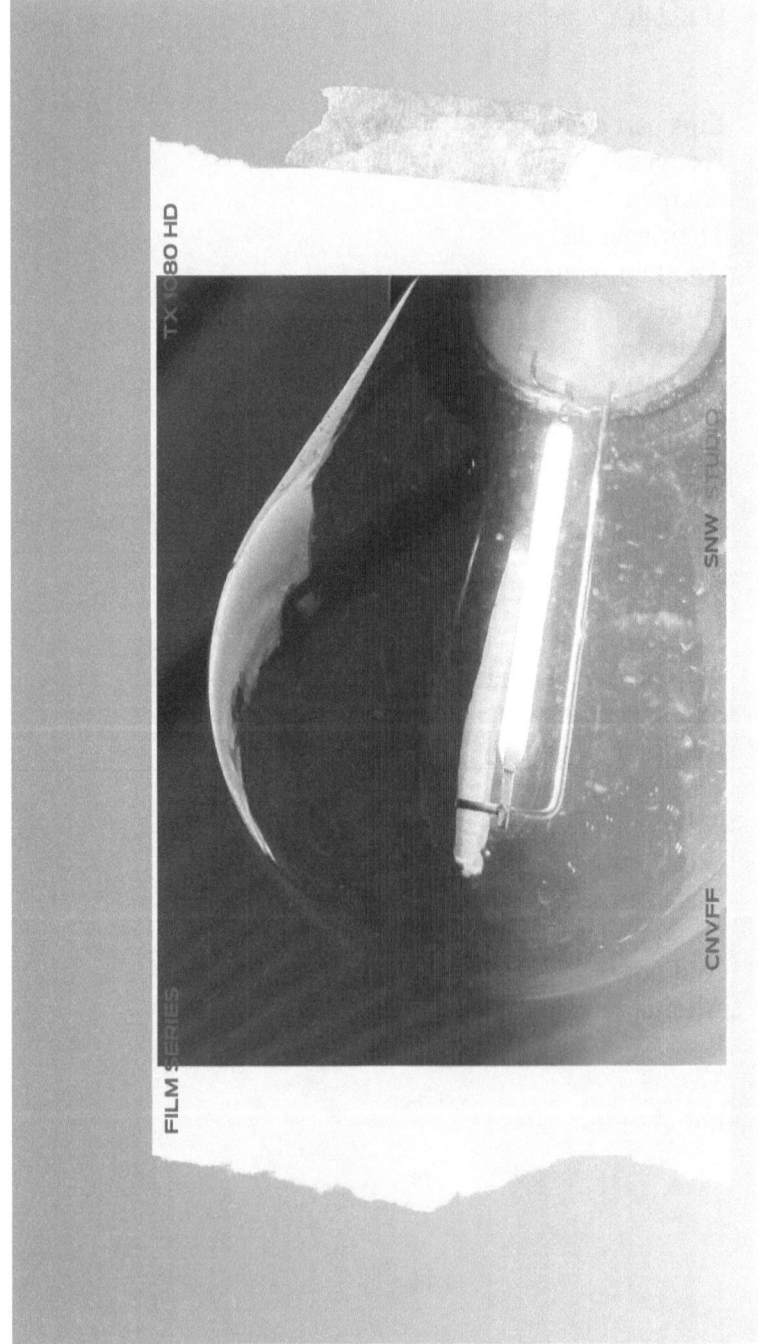

The Gardener

He went
Full
Scorched earth
But I'm a mother
You motherfucker
And I grow gardens
From ash
To nourish new seeds that
Slowly erupt
Into forests
That
Flood the grounds
With life
And
Fill the air
With hope

<u>A Pause</u>

My topography
And overgrown trails
Lead to hideaways
Closed off years before
For safety of
Preservation at best
It's a lonely frolic and
Destinations are lacking
I find myself alone
Where X marks the spot
And this bliss
Of unrestrained laughter
Bounces off
Impenetrable
Walls
To ricochet
Back to me
A chorus of silence that
Deafens
The perceptions
Of
Safety
Safety from
Crumbs of
Crumbling life blood
Scavenging
Hieroglyphics
In tongues
No one
Comprehends

This world is scandalous
And rigid
And fluid
And fine
A bit of a balance
To not crave
A gentle tiptoe to
That inevitable grave
That
Returns us all
To Stardust and memories
There is no safety
In
Solitude
Where passion subdued
Is exchange for
A lesser exchange
Of pain
For a moment

Good Mourning

Surplus

If your eyes
Overwhelm my senses
Render me senseless
What will I make of
Your fingertips?
Your caress?
I will need more skin
To handle your touch
And new language to
Release these
Sensations
Within
You evoke
Me
Awoke
Within me
I walk around with
Pieces of you
Embedded deep within
Hidden from no one
For they see my smile
And know
The origin
Of the banquet

Good Mourning

Mirage

Albeit cold
And silent
My bones swiftly summoned
Obey
To remain
By this seashore
I long for you
You know
I long for more
For long summer nights
With pause for pleasure
And steamed up
Sunglasses
Let them look
They'll roll on by
Like wisps of cotton clouds
That tease the blue skies
It fades
Quicker than I can take it
And leaves lose their
Green
While I lose my patience
And yet
I wait
You were here once
You know
And so was I

Good Mourning

Brenda Baker

<u>Provisions</u>

Shadows cast
Nonnegotiable
Pressure
As voices pause
And eyelids
Rest
Upon nothing
But
Bliss

Book of You

Already, I am
Here
Lolling about on your
Fringe tipped rug
Tracing outlines
Of patterned shapes
Woven deep
And tight
As you pour
The coffee
And I recite
From
My book of
You
Memories
That summoned your eyes
To my eyes
Your laugh to
My throat
And feet
That
Now rest close
Alert senses
To doors
Unlocked
And
Heartbeats
That deafen
Demands of reality
To a soft

Murmur
Like my voice
In your
Ear
Placing thoughts
Of things
You've only let roam free
In your mind's eye

Good Mourning

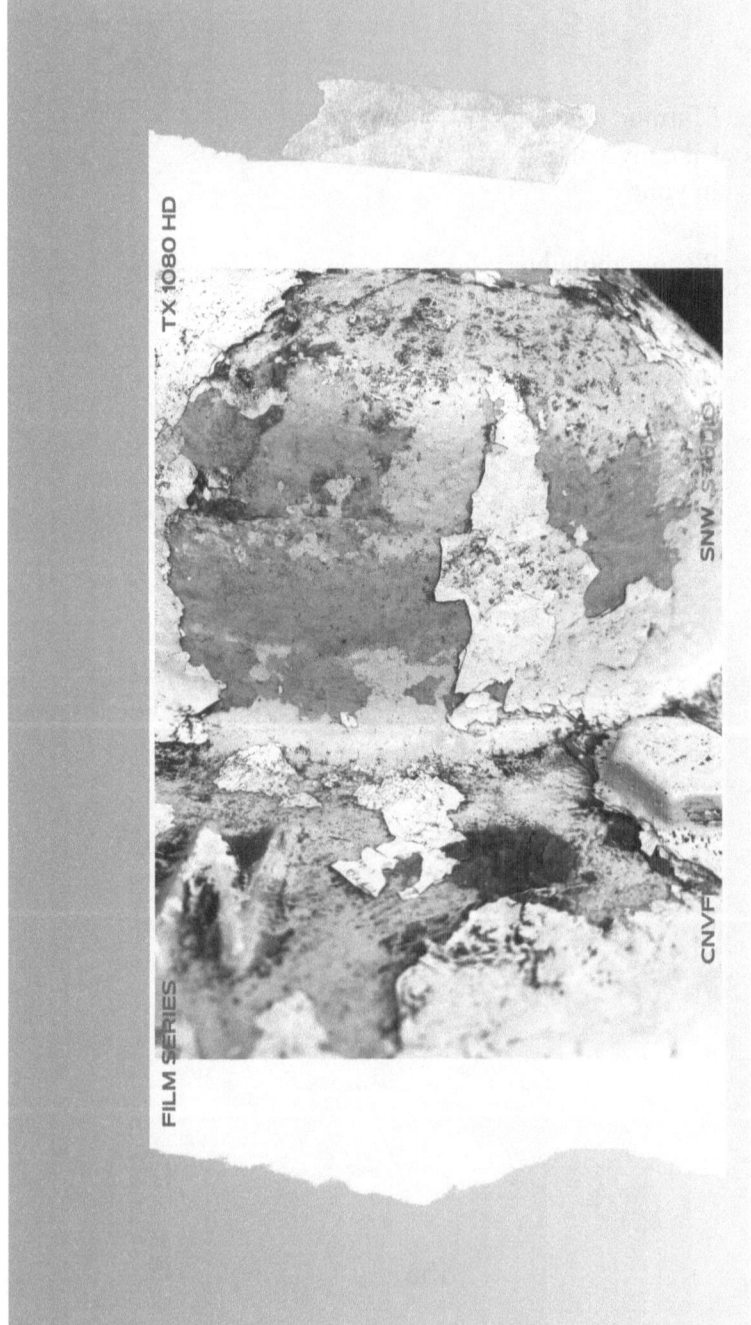

Repent

She sits idle
Idle hands carving statues
Like soap
A cradle for
A thorough ache
That holds tight
To memories
She prays
To wash clean
Willing sins down
The thirsty drain
While the song
Sticks firm
In her throat
Hands to neck
Hands in prayer
Hands flushed like cowards cheeks
That know how to deal
The deck
And split the skin
In cool morning mist

Captain

Do you know how to love her?
Do you know how to love such a soft
Force
That craves
Summer sunshine
In the dead of winter
While the sky floats dense
Soaked heavy with thick blankets
Of the season
And the forecast
Calls for rain
Do you know how to love her?
And stand witness
As she tiptoes
Through new fields
With caution strapped to her feet
And a map in her heart
With plans in her suitcase
Filled with options
To love her is to
Know
Your
Self
And choose to hold hands
With your own heart
'Til the final dip of the sun
Summons meaning
To the clouds above
As oceans roll on
Showcasing

A selection of everything
But her eyes have only
One selection
For partner
Ship
To sail these waters
And make it all
Feel like home

Good Mourning

Unearth

If I submerge
My beliefs
Into you
Will our timeline intertwine?
In due time
Will lips brush
Casually
Cautiously
Across eyelids
And dreams?
This unearthing of
Shadows
Shines dangerous
Beams
A tiny light
Pinpoints the night
Deep in crevices
That have yet to be seen
Breathe it in
Dip in deeper
Close your eyes
With senses deprived
Others spring to life
Like you
Before me

Good Mourning

Tiger Shark

If I sit
In the melancholy
It will call me
To swim
In pools
Of ink
And broken glass
And surpass
My patience
Of growth
In favor of
Blood in the water

Good Mourning

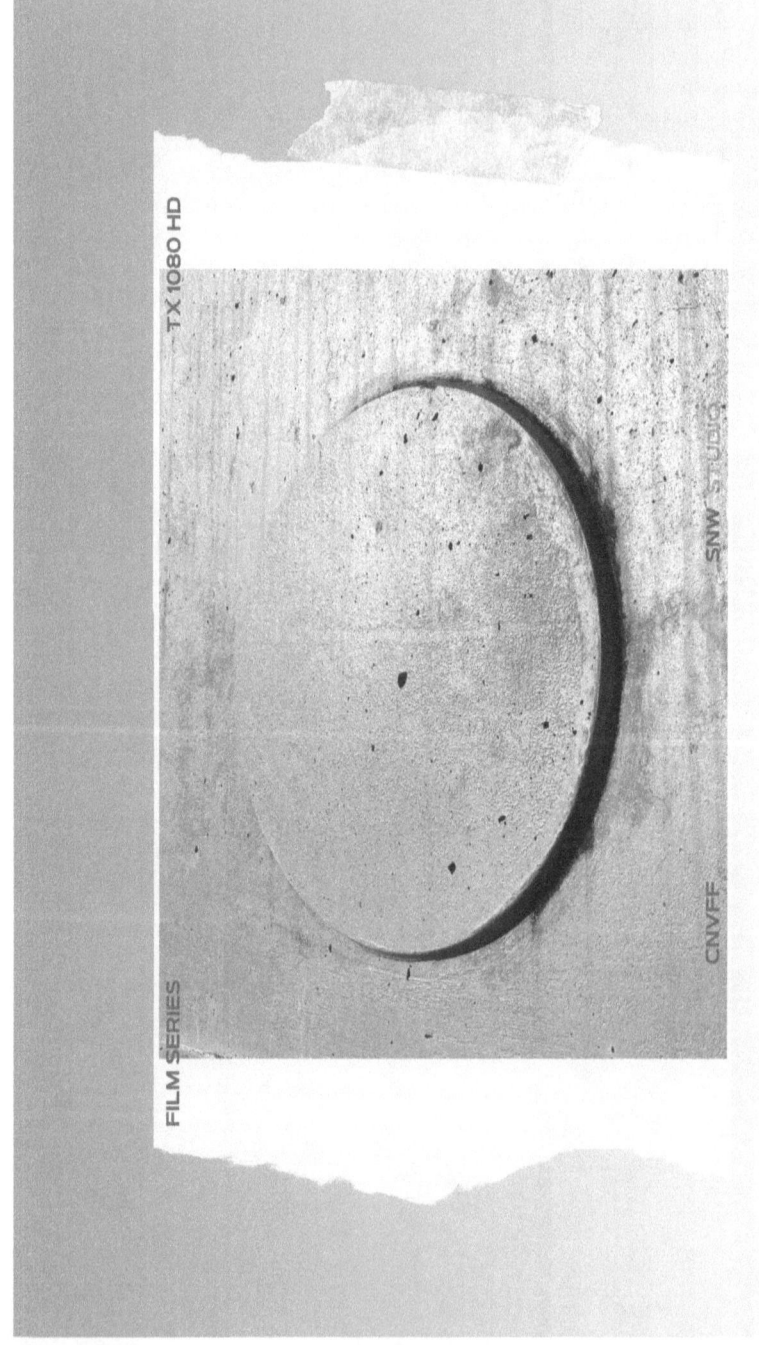

Silent Stories

Pleasantries exchanged
But eyes are sharp
And there are
Novels
Between the silence
Carving out
Time
To reminisce
Stories only
We
Know

The Dichotomy of You and Me

Murmur to me
Of this
Cognitive dissonance
That plagues your thoughts
As wild hands meet lips
With tongues that beg
For the menu
Do you
Then
Sleep restless in the nights
As I call your veins?
You know this
Invitation
Where time pauses
As seasons cease
Importance
While others call your name
I consume
Your presence
The dichotomy
Of
You and me
Tells tales from a past
We cannot
See
But this tensile
Strength
Has seen the feast
Has lost to famine
Is resurrected

Time and time
And time once more
To explore
New skin
And terrain
In splendid
Secret

Good Mourning

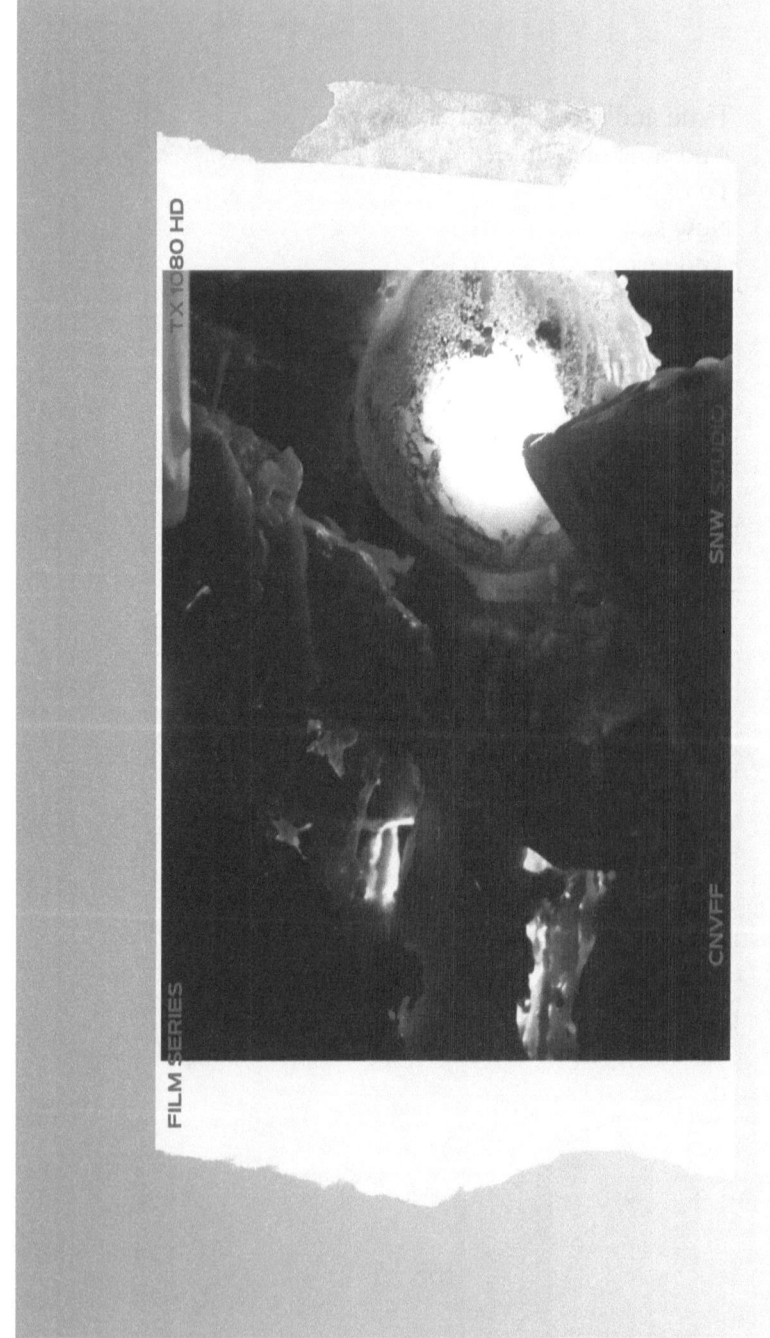

Candlelight

The war
It's over
Still
I'm still
A sensor
Of antenna nerves
And satellite ears
While sunsets prove
Another day of peace
But peace of mind
Is a mirage
When peripheral sight
Keeps track
Through the night
And the beast is known

www.ingramcontent.com/pod-product-compliance
Lightning Source LLC
Chambersburg PA
CBHW060606080526
44585CB00013B/708